Life Under the
Jim Crow Laws

by Charles George

Lucent Books, P.O. Box 289011, San Diego, CA 92198-9011

Titles in The Way People Live series include:

Life Among the Indian Fighters
Life During the Black Death
Life During the Great Depression
Life During the Renaissance
Life in a Japanese American
  Internment Camp
Life in Charles Dickens's England
Life in Communist Russia
Life in the American Colonies
Life in the Hitler Youth

Life in the North During the Civil War
Life in the South During the Civil War
Life of a Roman Slave
Life of a Slave on a Southern Plantation
Life on an African Slave Ship
Life on an Israeli Kibbutz
Life on Ellis Island
Life on the Underground Railroad
Life Under the Jim Crow Laws

Library of Congress Cataloging-in-Publication Data

George, Charles, 1949–
    Life under the Jim Crow laws / by Charles George.
    p.   cm. — (The way people live)
    Includes bibliographical references (p.   ) and index.
    SUMMARY: Discusses the background and effects of the Jim Crow laws
that were enacted after the Civil War to keep the races segregated.
    ISBN 1-56006-499-4 (lib. bdg. : alk. paper)
    1. Afro-Americans—Segregation—Southern States—History—19th
century Juvenile literature.   2. Afro-Americans—Segregation—Southern
States—History—20th century Juvenile literature.   3. Afro-Americans—
Civil rights—Southern States—History—19th century Juvenile literature.
4. Afro-Americans—Civil rights—Southern States—History—20th century
Juvenile literature.   5. Afro-Americans—Southern States—Social
conditions—19th century Juvenile literature.   6. Afro-Americans—
Southern States—Social conditions—20th century Juvenile literature.
7. Southern States—History—1865–1951 Juvenile literature.   8. Southern
States—Race relations Juvenile literature.   [1. Afro-Americans—History—
1877–1964.   2. Afro-Americans—Segregation.   3. Afro-Americans—Civil
rights.   4. Southern States—Race relations.]   I. Title.   II. Series.
    E185.61.G287   2000
    305.896075—dc21
                                                                99-32526
                                                                CIP

Contents

Discovering the Humanity in Us All

Books in The Way People Live series focus on groups of people in a wide variety of circumstances, settings, and time periods. Some books focus on different cultural groups, others, on people in a particular historical time period, while others cover people involved in a specific event. Each book emphasizes the daily routines, personal and historical struggles, and achievements of people from all walks of life.

To really understand any culture, it is necessary to strip the mind of the common notions we hold about groups of people. These stereotypes are the archenemies of learning. It does not even matter whether the stereotypes are positive or negative; they are confining and tight. Removing them is a challenge that's not easily met, as anyone who has ever tried it will admit. Ideas that do not fit into the templates we create are unwelcome visitors—ones we would prefer remain quietly in a corner or forgotten room.

The cowboy of the Old West is a good example of such confining roles. The cowboy was courageous, yet soft-spoken. His time (it is always a he, in our template) was spent alternatively saving a rancher's daughter from certain death on a runaway stagecoach, or shooting it out with rustlers. At times, of course, he was likely to get a little crazy in town after a trail drive, but for the most part, he was the epitome of inner strength. It is disconcerting to find out that the cowboy is human, even a bit childish. Can it really be true that cowboys would line up to help the cook on the trail drive grind coffee, just hoping he would give them a little stick of peppermint candy that came with the coffee shipment? The idea of tough cowboys vying with one another to help "Coosie" (as they called their cooks) for a bit of candy seems silly and out of place.

So is the vision of Eskimos playing video games and watching MTV, living in prefab housing in the Arctic. It just does not fit with what "Eskimo" means. We are far more comfortable with snow igloos and whale blubber, harpoons and kayaks.

Although the cultures dealt with in Lucent's The Way People Live series are often historically and socially well known, the emphasis is on the personal aspects of life. Groups of people, while unquestionably affected by their politics and their governmental structures, are more than those institutions. How do people in a particular time and place educate their children? What do they eat? And how do they build their houses? What kinds of work do they do? What kinds of games do they enjoy? The answers to these questions bring these cultures to life. People's lives are revealed in the particulars and only by knowing the particulars can we understand these cultures' will to survive and their moments of weakness and greatness.

This is not to say that understanding politics does not help to understand a culture. There is no question that the Warsaw ghetto, for example, was a culture that was brought about by the politics and social ideas of Adolf

Hitler and the Third Reich. But the Jews who were crowded together in the ghetto cannot be understood by the Reich's politics. Their life was a day-to-day battle for existence, and the creativity and methods they used to prolong their lives is a vital story of human perseverance that would be denied by focusing only on the institutions of Hitler's Germany. Knowing that children as young as five or six outwitted Nazi guards on a daily basis, that Jewish policemen helped the Germans control the ghetto, that children attended secret schools in the ghetto and even earned diplomas—these are the things that reveal the fabric of life, that can inspire, intrigue, and amaze.

Books in The Way People Live series allow both the casual reader and the student to see humans as victims, heroes, and onlookers. And although humans act in ways that can fill us with feelings of sorrow and revulsion, it is important to remember that "hero," "predator," and "victim" are dangerous terms. Heaping undue pity or praise on people reduces them to objects, and strips them of their humanity.

Seeing the Jews of Warsaw only as victims is to deny their humanity. Seeing them only as they appear in surviving photos, staring at the camera with infinite sadness, is limiting, both to them and to those who want to understand them. To an object of pity, the only appropriate response becomes "Those poor creatures!" and that reduces both the quality of their struggle and the depth of their despair. No one is served by such two-dimensional views of people and their cultures.

With this in mind, The Way People Live series strives to flesh out the traditional, two-dimensional views of people in various cultures and historical circumstances. Using a wide variety of primary quotations—the words not only of the politicians and government leaders, but of the real people whose lives are being examined—each book in the series attempts to show an honest and complete picture of a culture removed from our own by time or space.

By examining cultures in this way, the reader will notice not only the glaring differences from his or her own culture, but also will be struck by the similarities. For indeed, people share common needs—warmth, good company, stability, and affirmation from others. Ultimately, seeing how people really live, or have lived, can only enrich our understanding of ourselves.

Jim Crow: An American Disgrace

Jim Crow was the nickname given to a series of laws and customs practiced in the United States between the end of the Reconstruction era in 1877 and the early 1970s. They were designed to separate members of racial minorities—specifically African Americans—from mainstream white society and, therefore, to severely limit their participation in that society. This separation, and the discrimination that came with it, was particularly evident in transportation, housing, education, employment, and in the use of other public facilities.

Segregation, as these laws and practices were officially known, consisted of two types: de jure and de facto. De jure segregation was put in place and enforced by local, state, or federal laws. Every state that had been in the Confederacy during the Civil War, including Alabama, Arkansas, Florida, Georgia, Louisiana, Mississippi, North Carolina, South Carolina, Tennessee, Texas, and Virginia, passed such laws. In addition, other southern and so-called border states, such as Missouri, Kentucky, and Oklahoma, also placed legal restrictions on members of racial minorities.

De facto segregation existed (and in some cases still exists) not by law but by custom. This form of segregation involves the way one group of people treats another group of people. De facto segregation was not limited to the South; blacks and other minorities have encountered racial discrimination in almost every state.

Throughout history groups of people who considered themselves "superior," have tried to separate themselves from groups that they perceived as "inferior." In the United States many ethnic and religious groups have had to endure segregation. Roman Catholics, Jews, Irish Americans, Asian Americans, Mexican Americans, and Native Americans have all suffered the sting of exclusion and discrimination. Women and homosexuals have also had to bear this type of mistreatment.

However, in the century following the end of Reconstruction, African Americans became the primary targets of this unequal treatment at the hands of the white majority. The complex system of laws and customs that evolved in the Deep South, and to some extent in other regions of the country, became known as Jim Crow laws.

When and Where Were Jim Crow Laws Passed?

Although the customs of racial segregation and discrimination had their start much earlier, the first actual Jim Crow law was not passed until 1888, in Louisiana. This law, later copied in various other southern states, declared that blacks could not be seated with whites on railway cars.

Resistance to this first Jim Crow law began very soon. Homer Plessy, a light-skinned black man, purchased a first-class ticket on the East Louisiana Railway. When he tried to take his seat, he was ordered to the "colored" section. When he refused to comply, he was jailed. In court, Plessy argued that his civil rights, guaranteed under the Fourteenth Amendment to the U.S. Constitution, had been violated. His case was eventually heard by the U.S. Supreme Court. In its 1896 decision, the Court held that if Plessy "be a colored man and be so assigned, he has been deprived of no property, since he is not lawfully entitled to the reputation of being a white man."[1]

By this decision, known as *Plessy v. Ferguson*, the Court legally endorsed the practice of racial segregation. The Court stated that the Fourteenth Amendment to the Constitution (supposedly enacted to extend the

Who Was Jim Crow?

Jim Crow was not a real person. Most historians agree that he was originally a character in a song about a black man. Pulitzer Prize–winning historian Leon F. Litwack elaborates on the term in his definitive study of life in the Jim Crow South, *Trouble in Mind.*

"The term 'Jim Crow,' as a way of characterizing black people, had its origin . . . in the early nineteenth century. Thomas 'Daddy' Rice, a white minstrel, popularized the term. Using burned cork to blacken his face, attired in the ill-fitting, tattered garment of a beggar, and grinning broadly, Rice imitated the dancing, singing, and demeanor generally ascribed to Negro character. Calling it 'Jump Jim Crow,' he based the number on a routine he had seen performed in 1828 by an elderly and crippled Louisville stableman belonging to a Mr. Crow. 'Weel about, and turn about/ And do jis so;/ Eb'ry time I weel about,/ I jump Jim Crow.' The public responded with enthusiasm to Rice's caricature of black life. By the 1830s, . . . 'Jim Crow' had entered the American vocabulary, and many whites, northern and southern, came away from minstrel shows with their distorted images of black life, character, and aspirations reinforced. . . . Abolitionist newspapers employed the term in the 1840s to describe

separate railroad cars for blacks and whites in the North. But by the 1890s, 'Jim Crow' took on additional force and meaning to denote the subordination and separation of black people in the South."

Although Jim Crow was originally a character in a song, the term became synonymous with the segregation of black people.

rights enjoyed by white citizens to minorities) "could not have been intended to abolish distinctions based upon color, or to enforce social as distinguished from political equality."[2]

The Supreme Court's decision legally established a new idea in America—the concept of "separate but equal," meaning that states could legally segregate the races in public accommodations, such as railroad cars and public schools, as long as an effort was made to provide "equal" facilities for both races. In his majority opinion, Justice Henry Brown writes,

> We consider the underlying fallacy of the plaintiff's argument to consist in the assumption that the enforced separation of the two races stamps the colored race with a badge of inferiority. If this be so, it is not by reason of anything found in the act, but solely because the colored race chooses to put that construction upon it.[3]

The only Supreme Court justice who disagreed in this case was John Marshall Harlan. In his eloquent dissent, Harlan writes,

> The arbitrary separation of citizens, on the basis of race, while they are on a public highway, is a badge of servitude wholly inconsistent with the civil freedom and the equality before the law established by the Constitution. It cannot be justified upon any legal grounds.[4]

Justified or not, it would take sixty years before another Supreme Court would overturn the "separate but equal" doctrine.

After the initial laws were passed in Louisiana and other southern states, and especially after they were upheld by the Supreme Court, the floodgates opened. In the years following the *Plessy* decision, almost every former Confederate state passed additional segregation laws, giving the force of law to a racial system that had already become a fact of life in the South. By 1910 laws covering the smallest details of race relations were in place.

Why Were Jim Crow Laws Passed?

After the Civil War ended in 1865, whites in the defeated Confederacy were ordered by the U.S. government to integrate freed slaves into society on an equal basis. For a time, attempts were made along these lines by federally controlled Reconstruction governments, and equal rights—including the right to vote and hold office—were extended to freed slaves.

Federal troops stationed in the South enforced this equal opportunity for blacks until 1877. During these years, blacks began to exert a positive influence on the rebuilding of the South—so much so, in fact, that many whites worried that they would lose their status as superior to blacks. This was unacceptable to whites who considered themselves racially superior and resisted any evidence to the contrary.

When blacks began to demonstrate their competency in the use of political power, their success alarmed southern whites. "There was one thing," black educator W. E. B. Du Bois writes, "that the white South feared more than Negro dishonesty, ignorance, and incompetency, and that was Negro honesty, knowledge, and efficiency."[5]

With the end of Reconstruction in 1877, federal troops left the South. At that time, white opinion was divided on how blacks should be treated. The consensus in the South, though, was that blacks as a race were

In the South, Jim Crow laws were established that kept blacks segregated from whites in every aspect of life.

inferior to whites and should be put "in their place." Custom dictated the former slaves' position in society, but no laws existed to make those customs the official policy of southern states.

Between 1877 and 1887, lines between the races were gradually drawn. With passage of the first Jim Crow law in 1888, the "place" of blacks as an inferior race became recognized by states throughout the old Confederacy. By law, blacks' segregation from whites in every aspect of life became mandatory.

These laws were the result of fear and anger on the part of southern whites. Some feared that blacks would take their jobs, and many blamed blacks for the destruction and loss the Confederacy suffered as a result of the Civil War. Underlying the fear and anger was the refusal of most southern whites to accept blacks as equals.

Jim Crow Laws and the Social Fabric of the South

The Jim Crow laws were, in essence, statutes demanding the total segregation of blacks from whites and, therefore, affected almost every aspect of daily life for both races. They dictated segregation in churches, schools, housing, jobs, and public places. Blacks were segregated on all forms of public transportation, in sports and recreation, as well as in hospitals, orphanages, prisons, and asylums. Segregation was eventually extended to funeral homes, morgues, and cemeteries.

The races were not separated only by law. Even before the Civil War, social customs also kept the races apart in the South. As slaves, blacks had been expected to be subservient or face punishment. Since blacks were never considered equal to whites, they were expected to call all whites "master" and "mistress," speak only when spoken to, and never look a white person directly in the eye. Thus, a tradition of control of one race by another was established.

Because most white southerners believed in the superiority of the white race, they insisted that the long-standing social customs continue. As recently as the 1960s, blacks in the South were expected to address white people by "Mr.," "Mrs.," or "Miss," but whites called blacks by their first names. Blacks were also supposed to step aside when whites passed by them. Overall, whites felt, blacks would get along fine as long as they remembered "their place."

Was Segregation a New Idea?

Strict segregation of the races in the South occurred only after the Civil War. Before the war, whites and blacks were rarely segregated; by necessity black slaves lived in close proximity to the owners whose every wish they served. Even whites who owned no slaves had unquestioned authority over blacks. But with the end of slavery, some other means was needed to ensure the mastery of blacks by whites.

The History of Jim Crow

Jim Crow laws were an attempt by southern whites in the late 1800s and early 1900s to return blacks to their status of inferiority and servitude without actually calling it slavery. Behind this attempt was a belief that had existed for decades: Blacks, as a race, were inferior to whites. This belief, and the Jim Crow system that was based on it, would lead to almost a century of hatred and dissension between the races.

To understand fully what Jim Crow laws were and the effect they had on black people in the United States, it is necessary to understand how blacks were treated in the North and in the South before the laws were passed.

Before the Civil War

At the beginning of the nineteenth century, northern and southern citizens of the newly formed United States had settled into comfortable yet differing lifestyles. Because of the heavy dependence on slave labor by the cotton plantations of the South, different opinions about the morality of slavery evolved. There was less disagreement, however, on the need to control the actions of blacks, whether slave or free.

Northerners, for the most part, opposed slavery; in their own part of the country, however, the races were almost always segregated, and most northern whites supported such separation. Over 1 million free blacks lived in the North by the end of the Civil War. Most worked in unskilled jobs and lived in segregated sections of northern cities. Despite efforts to integrate into white society, most black northerners lived under legal and social restrictions. Blacks seldom lived, worked, or studied with whites. Although African Americans in the North were free, they did not enjoy the same rights as white citizens. Before 1870, for example, only five northern states, all in New England, freely allowed blacks to vote. In New York State, blacks were allowed to vote but were required to pay a poll tax that was not required of white voters.

Ironically, many whites from the pre–Civil War North were appalled at the familiarity tolerated and encouraged by southerners regarding their slaves. Historian C. Vann Woodward points out, "The supervision, maintenance of order, and physical and medical care of slaves necessitated many contacts and encouraged a degree of intimacy between the races unequaled, and often held distasteful, in other parts of the country."[6]

House servants in the South were often treated like members of the family. W. E. B. Du Bois, the Harvard-educated black leader of the late nineteenth and early twentieth centuries, describes this relationship in his classic work *The Souls of Black Folk*:

> Before and directly after the [Civil War], when all the best of the Negroes were domestic servants in the best of the white families, there were bonds of intimacy, affection, and sometimes blood relationship,

between the races. They lived in the same home, shared in the family life, often attended the same church, and talked and conversed with each other.[7]

It is doubtful, though, that such treatment extended beyond the household servants.

Regardless of the closeness of their relationships with whites, blacks were never considered equal to whites during these years. Blacks and whites might live together, work together, even laugh and cry together, but beneath all that closeness lay the disturbing truth that blacks were considered property.

Control over a slave's life was completely in the hands of the master. In *Growing Up Black in Rural Mississippi*, Chalmers Archer Jr. retells stories passed down by his aunts about life during and just after slavery: "Anyone's life as a slave is almost impossible to imagine. For someone else to have total control over your destiny is a continuous nightmare from which you never awaken unless freed."[8]

Before the Civil War, slaves dreamed of gaining their freedom. However, when the war brought an end to slavery, many found that freedom did not mean an end to white control over their lives. No one, black or white, knew exactly what to expect during the years to come.

After the Civil War

At first it appeared that radical change was in store for both blacks and whites. Before southern states could be readmitted to the Union, they had to ratify the Thirteenth Amendment to the U.S. Constitution, which officially abolished slavery in the United States.

Most southern whites accepted the Thirteenth Amendment with little resistance, but they did not expect the federal government to intervene any further in local affairs. According to historian Kenneth M. Stampp,

> [White southerners] assumed that the regulation of the freedmen would be left up to the individual states; and clearly most of them intended to replace slavery

Control over a slave's life was completely in the hands of the master, which sometimes meant the separation of mothers and their children.

Southern Homestead Act of 1867

When the Emancipation Proclamation freed the slaves in the former Confederate states, masters were not required to pay their slaves for past services or provide them even the barest aid. Author Joy Hakim, in her book, *Reconstruction and Reform*, quotes Frederick Douglass, one of the most influential black leaders of the nineteenth century, who wrote about the plight of the former slave.

"[The former slave] was free from the individual master, but the slave of society. He had neither money, property, nor friends. He was free from the old plantation, but he had nothing but the dusty road under his feet. . . . Old and young, sick and well, they were turned loose to the open sky, naked to their enemies."

Some Radicals believed voting rights were not enough. They felt newly freed blacks needed economic assistance to get on their feet. The Southern Homestead Act, passed by Congress in 1867, opened public lands in the South to blacks and whites loyal to the Union. The act was intended to put freed slaves to work on land of their own. However, because freed blacks were poor, they did not have even the small amount of money required to purchase the land—less than a dollar an acre. Consequently, the act failed to achieve its purpose and most of the land was bought by speculators, lumber companies, and large plantation owners.

with a caste system that would keep the Negroes perpetually subordinate to the whites. Negroes were to remain a dependent laboring class; they were to be governed by a separate code of laws; they were to play no active part in the South's political life; and they were to be segregated socially.[9]

As a means of controlling their former slaves, many states from the old Confederacy passed so-called Black Codes.

The Black Codes

To put it bluntly, the Black Codes placed blacks in a sort of twilight zone between slavery and freedom. In South Carolina, for example, blacks were prohibited from working in any job other than agriculture without obtaining a permit. Louisiana required all black farm laborers to sign a contract with the landholder during the first days of January. This contract was binding for the entire calendar year, and blacks were then not allowed to leave their place of employment without the landowner's permission. Several states provided that "blacks found without lawful employment were to be arrested as vagrants and auctioned off or hired to landholders who would pay their fines."[10]

Although the codes guaranteed some rights, such as legalizing black marriages, allowing blacks to own property, and the right to sue and be sued, the main purpose was to restrict blacks' civil rights. Interracial marriages, ownership or possession of firearms, serving on juries, and testifying against white men were all prohibited.

Carl Schurz, a Republican senator from Missouri from 1869 until becoming Secretary of the Interior in 1877, considered the Black Codes to be merely another form of slavery. To him, these laws were "a striking embodiment of the idea that although the former owner has lost his individual right of property in the former slave, the blacks at large belong to the whites at large."[11]

Without some intervention from Washington, the South seemed intent upon restoring its former social system. The year 1866 brought sweeping changes, however.

Congressional Reconstruction

In the nation's congressional elections of 1866, a group known as the Radical Republicans won decisive victories. They controlled every northern state and gained a two-thirds majority in both the House of Representatives and the Senate. Outraged by the arrogance of southern states in their treatment of former slaves, Congress outlawed the Black Codes, established the Committee of Reconstruction to hear testimony about violence and cruelty toward freed slaves, and established the Freedmen's Bureau to provide aid to 4 million freed slaves.

In addition, Congress passed the Civil Rights Act of 1866, declaring blacks to be citizens under the law and denying states any power to restrict their rights. President Andrew Johnson, a former slaveowner and a firm believer in keeping blacks subservient to whites, vetoed the bill. Congress overrode the veto, and the bill was passed into law. Under its provisions, federal troops were ordered to remain in the South to enforce the new law.

Congress also took control of Reconstruction. Under the Congressional Reconstruction plan, a southern state could only regain full admittance to the Union by adopting a new state constitution that allowed blacks to vote and by accepting the Fourteenth Amendment, which was ratified in 1868 and guaran-

Blanche K. Bruce and Civil Rights

The first black person to serve a full term in the U.S. Senate, Blanche K. Bruce (1841–1898), represented Mississippi from 1875 to 1881 and took a special interest in civil rights issues. In 1880 Bruce, who had been born a slave, spoke out in support of a House bill protecting the civil rights and extending the opportunities of Native Americans. His remarks addressed the subject of the general meaning of the American experience: "As a people, our history is full of surmounted obstacles. We have been scaling difficult problems for more than a hundred years. We have been (and will continue to be) settling material, moral, and great political questions that before our era had been unsolved."

Blanche K. Bruce was the first black person to serve a full term in the U.S. Senate.

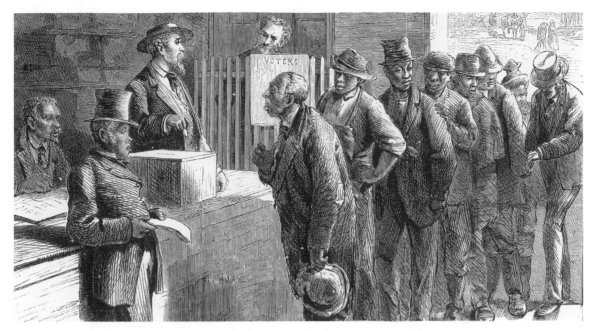

The passage of the Fifteenth Amendment to the Constitution in 1870 gave black men the right to vote.

teed adult black men citizenship and equal protection under the law. Two years later, in 1870, Congress further clarified its position by passing the Fifteenth Amendment, which specifically guaranteed black citizens the right to vote. Congress's attempt to give full rights to African Americans in the South would, unfortunately, be short-lived.

The leader of the Radical Republicans, Thaddeus Stevens, summed up their philosophy when he stated that the goal of Reconstruction was to give blacks perfect equality before the law and "to overcome the prejudice and ignorance and wickedness which resisted such reform."[12]

Under Congressional Reconstruction, southerners were required to look upon slaves in an entirely different way—as equals. Having always believed that blacks were inferior, whites were bound to resent being told they had to share privileges they had previously taken for granted.

To many blacks, it seemed as though their former masters did not know how to relate to them. Chalmers Archer Jr., who grew up in rural Mississippi, recounts how his family's matriarch, Mama Jane, regarded the changes brought about in the lives of blacks after the Civil War:

[Black] people experienced much less overt racism right after slavery ended. It was as if white people were trying to make up for the wrongs they had inflicted on us during the two hundred and forty-six years of slavery. Not that all white people of that era were kind and benevolent to black people. There were always bands of marauding renegade whites who attacked black families without reason and many innocent people were killed. They seemed to want to take out their frustrations of having lost the war on black people.[13]

Thaddeus Stevens

One of the most outspoken and influential public figures of the nineteenth century was the Republican senator from Pennsylvania, Thaddeus Stevens (1792–1868). He worked tirelessly for civil rights and equality under the law for all races. His strong opinions meant that people either admired him greatly or hated him.

Growing up in Vermont, he learned to say exactly what he thought. He was fiercely honest, had an amazing intellect, and strong, handsome features. When he was twenty-four, he moved to Gettysburg, Pennsylvania, where he became a lawyer.

Stevens's passion was the abolition of slavery. Long before the Civil War, he supported efforts to rid the nation of this so-called "peculiar institution." As a senator, he wrote civil rights laws, coauthored the Fourteenth Amendment to the Constitution, and led Congress in preparing the Fifteenth Amendment.

With the end of the Civil War, Stevens believed the southern states should be forced to allow blacks to vote. As a leader of the Radical Republicans, he opposed President Andrew Johnson's policies toward the South, which seemed to favor former Confederates while standing against blacks and northerners.

Even after his death in 1868, Thaddeus Stevens made his opinions known. After lying in state in the Capitol, he was buried in a cemetery where blacks and whites rested side by side, unusual in the North at that

Thaddeus Stevens fought tirelessly to give blacks complete equality to whites under the law.

time. In her book, *Reconstruction and Reform,* Joy Hakim writes that on his tombstone, his own words stated that he had chosen that resting place to illustrate the principles by which he had lived.

> "I repose in this quiet and secluded
>   spot,
> Not from any natural preference for
>   solitude
> But, finding other Cemeteries limited as
>   to Race by Charter Rules,
> I have chosen this that I might illustrate
>   in my death
> The Principles which I advocated
> Through a long life."

To Mama Jane, Archer suggests, there were two reasons why whites improved their treatment of blacks right after the Civil War ended:

[There] was a definite fear by whites that the federal troops might intervene if they became too violent toward blacks. But more likely, many whites who had once been rich, powerful plantation owners found themselves pauper poor like the newly freed slaves. Homes were burned and crops ruined or not harvested when blacks could not or would not work for their "masters" near the end of the war.[14]

Freedom for slaves, then, meant economic ruin for many whites who were left with no workers to tend crops and no money to hire freed blacks to continue that work. Resentment over being left financially vulnerable built steadily as the presence of federal troops dictated acceptance of blacks' new status in society.

As time passed, whites realized something had to be done to put blacks back "in their place." That chance came when federal troops left the South in 1877. Attempts by whites to repay blacks for years of slavery soon gave way to a new era, one in which race relations were characterized by segregation and discrimination.

The Rise of the "Redeemers"

After more than ten years of Reconstruction, the American public seemed to lose interest in the plight of the former slaves. By the mid-1870s, many Radical Republicans, including Stevens, had died, and the nation's attention was focused on westward expansion. The years of Reconstruction had seen the gradual rise to power in southern states of conservative white Democrats. In 1877 Republicans, seeing their influence waning, made a compromise with southern Democrats, resulting in the withdrawal of federal troops from the South and a return to "home rule." Reconstruction was officially at an end.

After Reconstruction, in spite of the Fourteenth and Fifteenth Amendments, blacks were denied equal civil and political rights. Southern states developed clever ways to get around the language of both amendments. In addition, between 1883 and 1896, the Supreme Court and Congress invalidated or repealed many of the measures that had been passed during Reconstruction. Coupled with the *Plessy v. Ferguson* decision allowing social segregation, blacks were only half emancipated.

For the next ten years, neither whites nor blacks had any real guidelines on how they should behave toward each other. In *Race Relations in Virginia,* researcher Charles E. Wynes notes, "The most distinguishing factor in the complexity of social relations between the races was that of inconsistency. From 1870 to 1900, there was no generally accepted code of racial mores."[15]

With control of the South in conservative Democratic hands, southerners said their region had been "redeemed." So-called redeemer governments of southern states, controlled by former leaders of the Confederacy, quickly moved to again rewrite state constitutions. Southern whites began establishing a system in defiance of federal law to disenfranchise blacks. According to one historian, "The South refused to forget and forgive those years of humiliation when Negroes came close to winning equality."[16] And that humiliation could be overcome by bringing back as much of the Old South's way of life as possible. One tactic that was effective in keeping blacks subservient was to terrorize and coerce them.

Terror as a Tool of the Redeemers

While some southern whites pursued legal means to undo the effects of Reconstruction, others formed hate groups such as the Ku Klux Klan (KKK) to help them regain their old way of life. These groups waged campaigns of terrorism and hatred toward blacks. Any whites brave enough to defend blacks were also targets of harassment.

Violence soon became the first resort of whites determined to regain control of southern

Hate groups such as the Ku Klux Klan began a reign of terror and violence to keep blacks subservient and bring back the "Old South's" way of life.

governments. Using terrorist tactics borrowed from the KKK and other secret groups, conservatives in Mississippi, for example, resolved to use whatever means necessary, including violence, to regain control of their state in the elections of 1875. Their actions were copied in other states, and this blueprint for influencing elections became known as the Mississippi Plan.

Prior to the 1875 elections, whites organized private militia groups, armed themselves with rifles, and paraded through areas of heavy black population. Members of some groups carried so-called dead-books containing the names of black leaders. Such lists

were designed to intimidate black leaders into abandoning their attempts to gain equality and justice. In addition, these reactionary militia groups broke up Republican Party meetings to intimidate the few southern whites who supported equality for blacks. As election day neared, white activists provoked riots in Memphis and New Orleans in which hundreds of blacks died. Likewise, armed guards were posted at voter registration locations to prevent blacks from registering to vote.

The plan of violence and intimidation proved to be effective. As one historian writes,

On election day, thousands of terrified Negroes were hiding in the swamps or staying in their cabins. In some places the only Negroes who could vote were those who showed Democratic ballots or who were accompanied to the polls by white men. Many who were bold enough to carry Republican ballots were fired upon or driven away from the polls.[17]

The Mississippi Plan, which was carried out in some fashion in most southern states, effectively ended the short period of political influence enjoyed by blacks in the South. Deprived of representation in government, African Americans were powerless to resist a flood of Jim Crow laws designed to limit their rights.

These new laws were strict and far reaching. Almost no aspect of life in the South was unaffected. According to historian C. Vann Woodward, the Jim Crow laws

were comparable with the black codes of the old regime, though the laxity that mitigated the harshness of the black codes was replaced by a rigidity that was more typical of the segregation code. That code lent the sanction of law to a racial ostracism that extended to churches and

In the South, militia groups armed themselves with rifles to intimidate and prevent blacks from voting.

The Ku Klux Klan

What began in 1865 as a harmless social club for Confederate veterans did not stay harmless for long. Formed in Pulaski, Tennessee, in response to the boredom of small-town life, the Ku Klux Klan (KKK) soon brought terror to the South.

Six young men formed the organization. Their goal was to keep it secret and make it as outrageous as possible, partly for the fun of it and partly to avoid any military or political implications, which would have attracted unwanted attention from federal authorities. The flowing white sheets and pointed hoods they wore, and the names of Klan officers—grand cyclops, grand magi, grand turk, night hawk, and lictor—were chosen for amusement. Shortly after the KKK's founding, its members decided to show off by riding through town in the middle of the night. Soon other former Confederates asked to join.

During 1866 members of the club discovered that their activities produced a chilling effect on local blacks. Hooded night riders making late-night visits to black homes were seen by blacks as real threats. Threats evolved into violence against those blacks who insisted on standing up for their newly acquired rights.

Eventually the KKK became a deadly serious organization of terror and intimidation, its members riding across the South until late 1869. Then, because of pressure from Reconstruction governments, the organization disbanded and its leaders were hunted down and jailed. Tough anti-Klan laws were passed.

Early in the twentieth century, though, the Klan was reborn as a patriotic fraternal organization and became a part of life throughout the country in the 1920s. In 1925, at the height of its power, forty thousand hooded and robed Klansmen marched down the streets of Washington, D.C., as a demonstration of strength.

Whether a secret terrorist group or a public "benevolent society," its effect was the same. Even today, its members espouse hatred of all nonwhites, Catholics, immigrants, Jews, homosexuals, and any others they feel threaten their way of life. Although the Federal Bureau of Investigation and state authorities continue to watch the Klan, it still retains the ability to frighten the targets of its hatred.

schools, to housing and jobs, to eating and drinking. Whether by law or by custom, that ostracism extended to virtually all forms of public transportation, to sports and recreations, to hospitals, orphanages, prisons, and asylums, and ultimately to funeral homes, morgues, and cemeteries. The new Southern system was regarded as the "final settlement," the "return to sanity," the "permanent system."[18]

In order to assure white supremacy in every aspect of life—social, spiritual, political, and economic—blacks had to be relegated by law to second-class citizenship. The Jim Crow era was born.

Daily Life Under Jim Crow

As more and more Jim Crow laws were passed, blacks were gradually and systematically separated from whites. The message from southern whites to blacks seemed clear: If you want to be free, do it somewhere else. And if you want to stay here, you had better follow *our* rules!

One historian effectively summarizes the life of blacks, both adults and children, under the Jim Crow laws:

> Negroes . . . were either excluded from railway cars, omnibuses, stagecoaches, and steamboats or assigned to special "Jim Crow" sections; they sat, when permitted, in secluded and remote corners of theaters and lecture halls; they could not enter most hotels, restaurants, and resorts, except as servants; they prayed in "Negro pews" in the white churches, and if partaking of the sacrament of the Lord's Supper, they waited until all the whites had been served the bread and wine. Moreover, they were often educated in segregated schools, punished in segregated prisons, nursed in segregated hospitals, and buried in segregated cemeteries.[19]

Even though the laws generally required that separate facilities for blacks should be equal to those of whites, no real effort was made to comply with that mandate. Every effort was made, however, to ensure that blacks were kept separate from whites in every aspect of daily life. When contact between the races was necessary, such as on the job or on

As more Jim Crow laws passed, blacks were assigned special sections on trains, buses, stagecoaches, and steamboats.

the street, certain strict rules of etiquette applied. Most of these rules made it clear that, in the eyes of whites, blacks were not respected members of society.

A Matter of Respect

One of the most basic methods people use to convey respect is in the way they address each other when meeting. Most southern whites, in that situation, refused to address blacks as "Mr." or "Mrs." With few exceptions, blacks, no matter what their age, could expect to be called by their first names, even by very young whites. Occasionally whites would call certain black individuals by their last names only. This was regarded by southern whites as a way to show some limited amount of respect. Blacks were not even supposed to use titles of respect such as "Mr." and "Mrs." with each other, especially in the presence of whites. This pressure on blacks was so strong that they often referred to each other instead as "Brother Smith" or "Sister Jones."

At the heart of reserving "Mr." and "Mrs." for use with whites was the belief that blacks could never be equals with whites. One lawyer from Virginia explained that he could not address a black man as "Mr." because he would be recognizing the black as an equal. He said, furthermore, that he could not think much of his own title after calling a black man by it.

A black male whose name was not known was called "Boy" if young and "Uncle" if old. A young black woman was "Girl," or hailed anonymously as "You, there," or something just as vague, if her first name was not known. An older black woman was "Auntie." Southern whites considered these to be titles of address that did not imply prejudice. Whites in authority, however—petty offici-

als, police, overseers, and similar persons—simply and bluntly used the term *nigger*.

One account of the social customs encountered by blacks in the days of Jim Crow was written by Elizabeth Delany, who, along with her sister, Sarah, grew up in North Carolina. They later moved to New York City and became a teacher and a dentist, respectively. Both were over one hundred years old when they completed their memoirs, *Having Our Say: The Delany Sisters' First One Hundred Years*, in which Elizabeth Delany recalls,

> When I was a child, the words used to describe us most often were colored, Negro, and nigger. I've also been called jigger-boo, pickaninny, coon—you name it, honey. Some of these words are worse than others, and how mean they are depends on who is saying them and why.[20]

In addition to forms of address, other rules of conduct existed between blacks and whites. Physical contact between the races was particularly regulated, and any violation of the "rules" by blacks usually brought swift retribution.

Double Standards

Today it is common for people to greet each other with a handshake or an embrace. But during the decades of Jim Crow, blacks could not expect whites to shake their hands and were not supposed to embarrass whites by extending a hand in greeting. This taboo was primarily designed to prevent black men from coming into physical contact with white women, but it applied almost as strictly to shaking hands with men of different races.

One historian illustrated the importance of this social restriction by recalling an event that took place in Columbus, Georgia, during the early decades of the twentieth century. Five white men kidnapped three black schoolboys at gunpoint on the city's streets.

After being driven to a secluded spot, the boys were asked whether the white speakers who had appeared at the Negro high school during Brotherhood Week had shaken hands with the school's Negro principal. When the boys insisted they didn't know, they were stripped naked, severely flogged, and forced to run for their lives while the men took pot-shots at their heels.[21]

In addition to having to be careful in the way they greeted whites on the street, black people also had to obey strict rules of etiquette when visiting white people's homes. They were expected to go to the back door of a white person's house rather than the front door. It was considered impudent and insulting for a black man or woman to knock on the front door of a white person's house, or even ring the doorbell, no matter their social, professional, or economic standing.

Many southern whites, on the other hand, felt they could open the door of any black person's home and walk in without knocking. Besides entering uninvited, many whites felt they were allowed to make themselves at home without asking the black homeowner. According to one study of racial attitudes during the Jim Crow era, "When they [whites] fail to wipe their feet and 'slosh mud over the

A Cruel Southern "Sport"

A young white southerner from Birmingham, Alabama, in an article originally written for *Southern Exposure* magazine and later published in editor Chris Mayfield's book *Growing Up Southern,* describes the southern "sport" they called "nigger-knocking."

"Nigger-knocking, like fighting to bring blood, was a phenomenon of my freshman year in high school, . . . a regular Sunday night ritual after Methodist Youth Fellowship. We would gather behind the church, usually in a group of four or five—four being the ideal number, since everyone could then have his own [car] window.

Next to rocks and [pieces of clay flower] pots, water balloons were probably our most popular munitions. They were relatively harmless—or at least not potentially fatal. They could, when thrown from a car at forty miles an hour, stun with a direct hit and produce a grand fallout area even with a miss.

But probably the subtlest, most accurate, and most imaginative weapon of all was the simplest and easiest to use. Automobile radio aerials [antennae] were no trouble to steal and could be carried in a ready position almost invisibly and discarded instantly if need be. The only trouble with aerials, though, was finding proper quarry [an unsuspecting black pedestrian]. The object, of course, was to find game walking close enough to the street, since the aerial's reach was, unfortunately, a bit limited. And one had to be accurate enough to avoid necks and faces, since that would be *too* cruel at forty or fifty miles an hour. At any rate, when a target was found, all that was needed was a wrist movement, and the aerial would be extended perpendicular to the car, back high, and would hit with a resounding splat that could draw blood from a bare back and raise, we were sure, delicious whelts on a covered one."

floors' of Negro homes, it is interpreted by the Negroes as assuming that all Negro homes are dirty and a little more dirt won't hurt."[22]

Since black homes were almost always located in undesirable areas of town (commonly referred to as "the Bottoms," "the Flats," or simply "Niggertown"), and because sanitary conditions in those areas were invariably poor, many whites assumed that black homes were not worthy of respect. James Robinson, who grew up in such a section of Knoxville, Tennessee, describes the houses in which blacks lived as "hardly more than rickety shacks clustered on stilts like Daddy Long Legs along the slimy bank of putrid and evil-smelling 'Cripple Creek.'" Surrounded by a slaughterhouse, a foundry, and tobacco warehouses, in addition to the foul-smelling creek, the neighborhood was "a world set apart and excluded."[23]

Most blacks knew what was expected of them when visiting whites' homes. One southern black man explains how he coped with this situation:

> When I go to a white man's house I stand in the yard and yell, and wait for him to come to the door. If he tells me to come, then I go up to the door and talk to him, but I don't go in unless he tells me. If he tells me, then I go in; but I don't sit down unless he tells me.[24]

It was considered improper for a black person to sit down in the living room or den of a white home. This rule applied whether the person was visiting or employed as a servant in the house. Blacks were expected to do any necessary sitting in the kitchen or in their own quarters, if they had them. Some whites were so adamant about the taboo that they would actually remove a chair that had been used by a black person in their home and sometimes even burn it. At the same time, southern etiquette allowed whites to feel free to sit anywhere in a black person's home without waiting for an invitation.

Black men were also expected to take off their hats when entering a white person's home or place of business or when meeting whites on the street. Not to do so was considered rude and uppity and could bring severe repercussions. White men, on the other hand, rarely took off their hats as a show of courtesy. One black Mississippian put it this way: "These peckerwoods for the most part don't like to give respect to the Negro's home. There are some of them that come here and talk till times gets better, but they never show any courtesy. They wouldn't pull off their hats if they had to."[25]

Each of these social customs was imposed on black people, and they had little choice but to comply. However, southern whites required more than just obedience to the system; they wanted blacks to seem happy about it. It was not enough merely to observe the letter of the social ritual. So that they would not appear sassy or sullen, blacks also had to demonstrate, by tone of voice and mannerisms, that they were willingly and cheerfully being humble.

Public Places

In public places especially, blacks were required to behave in certain ways, and some public places were completely off-limits to blacks. They suffered constant humiliation whenever they tried to enter public buildings or parks, whether for entertainment, official business, health care, or worship. They were segregated at practically all public meetings in rural areas of the South, especially at assemblies in public auditoriums. If allowed to

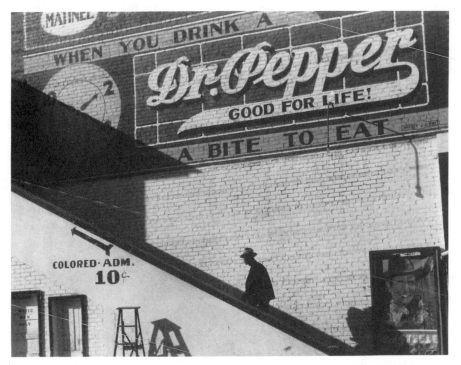

Theaters were a primary source of amusement for both blacks and whites during the Jim Crow era. However, blacks bought their tickets at a side window and had to sit in their "special" segregated section of the theater.

use a town's public auditorium for some event (a guest speaker or a graduation ceremony from an all-black school, for example) blacks would not be surprised to arrive at the auditorium and find the doors to facilities such as toilets locked.

The primary sources of amusement in the South, for whites and blacks alike during the Jim Crow era, were motion-picture theaters, swimming pools, skating rinks, bowling alleys, dance halls, and baseball fields. In virtually every southern city and town, blacks were either completely banned from using these facilities or were severely restricted in their access to them.

Blacks could attend motion-picture theaters in most towns partly because white owners could not afford to close their doors to the blacks' patronage. Seating in all theaters was strictly segregated, however. A black domestic worker in Marked Tree, Arkansas, recalls her experience:

Colored [people] go upstairs in the movie here. It is either too hot or too cold up there. Colored buy tickets at the side window. You just stand there, as a rule, until all the white people go in. When they fill up downstairs some of the white fellows come up and set with the colored. Most of the time they are just young fellows. Sometimes they come up with their girl friends. It's just like it always is—the white can come on your side, but you don't go on theirs.[26]

In the South, school playgrounds, ballparks, and fairgrounds were usually reserved for whites. Play facilities were not provided for black schoolchildren at public expense, and it was not possible for them to share in the use of equipment intended for white children. Blacks who sought space for recreation or picnics resorted to churchyards, vacant lots, or open fields.

Virtually all the public swimming areas in the segregated South were reserved for whites, including those built and operated with tax money paid by both races. This meant nonwhites were forbidden from entering the surf at Miami Beach or any of the South's other famous public beaches. In a few instances, remote and relatively undeveloped spots were made available to nonwhite bathers. One exception to this exclusion existed, at times, for black women. They could enter a white beach, but only if they were accompanied by a white infant under their care.

Other outdoor spaces were similarly segregated. It was not uncommon to find signs at the entrances to public parks proclaiming "Negroes and Dogs Not Allowed." In 1902 a black mother from the South wrote to a national magazine, expressing her dismay at the so-called separate-but-equal facilities she had encountered:

> Many colored women, who wash, iron, scrub, cook, or sew all the week to help pay the rent . . . and help fill the many small mouths, would deny themselves some of the necessities of life if they could take their little children and teething babies on the cars to the parks of a Sunday afternoon and sit under the trees, enjoy the cool breezes and breathe God's pure air for only two or three hours; but this is denied them. Some of the parks have signs, "No Negroes allowed on these grounds except as servants." Pitiful, pitiful customs and laws that make war on women and babies! There is no wonder that we die; the wonder is that we persist in living.[27]

Besides parks and other public facilities, retail businesses were also strictly segregated. Blacks were severely restricted when it came to eating in restaurants and buying clothing in department stores.

Something to Eat

The taboo against interracial dining was pronounced in the South. Many restaurants would not serve blacks at all, and those that did frequently reserved a side or back entrance for blacks, or served them at a table in the kitchen. Blacks could sometimes buy a sandwich and a drink at lunch counters and roadside stands, but they had to eat some distance away.

As late as the 1950s and 1960s, in the waning days of the Jim Crow era, many white owners of southern eating establishments found ways to continue their discriminatory practices despite new civil rights laws. In an effort to discourage black patronage, restaurant managers, waiters, or cooks sometimes made the food served to minorities inedible by filling it with salt, pepper, or even chemicals that caused violent stomach cramps and vomiting. Incidents were also reported in which bartenders and hotel managers, after serving black customers, would make a show of smashing their drinking glasses so that they would not be used later by white customers.

A young black teacher recalled one such incident that occurred in the 1940s when she and a companion visited a fairly exclusive restaurant:

> We ordered the same thing—something *en casserole*. We waited almost an hour before it arrived. Both he and I noticed it looked peculiar and different from the same dish served other places. When we cut into it there was a hard crust of browned salt about one-half inch thick on

top. Naturally, the salt had gone through and the stuff couldn't be eaten. I looked at my friend and he caught my look. We were aware that the waiters and managers were watching us to see what we would do. We pretended to be discussing something else and we decided we would not send it back, as they might remove the crust of salt and add something worse—you know they will spit in food. I've heard that from kitchen help. We decided to eat what we could and pretend to enjoy it. That was what they didn't want us to do, so we'd be game enough to spoil their fun. It was awful plowing through that food, but we did. They looked amazed when they removed our dishes. They then served our dessert, which appeared and tasted all right. The entire day was spoiled.[28]

Something to Buy

When black people in the age of Jim Crow wanted to go shopping, their choice of stores was as limited as their choice of restaurants. There were stores that they could enter, and there were some they could not. Once inside, black customers were frequently limited in what they could do and what products they could buy.

In Baltimore, Maryland, for example, few of the leading department stores encouraged the trade of African Americans. The stores in that city, like ones in many other U.S. cities both in the North and the South, either refused service to blacks altogether or allowed them to buy items only from certain counters. If the store allowed blacks to shop, it sometimes denied them the privilege of trying on items such as dresses, hats, or gloves. In stores that refused service, a floorwalker approached black patrons upon their entrance and advised them that the store did not cater to "Negro trade."

Jim Bishop, the author of a 1971 biography of Martin Luther King Jr., writes that King had grown up in an affluent middle-class family, was respected and treated politely in his own neighborhood, but was dismayed by the treatment he received when he went shopping. King's treatment at the hands of white sales clerks was typical of the Jim Crow era:

> On those occasions when he went downtown to buy something, he was a "nigger," one who would not be waited on in a store when his turn came, the butt of short tempers and acidulous [harsh] tongues when he didn't make up his mind quickly or took too long reaching into his trouser pocket for money. . . . In the heat of summer, he could not buy a Coca-Cola in a five-and-ten-cent store, nor could he use the sparkling water fountain in a white park.[29]

Something to Read

Eating and shopping in white-owned establishments were difficult for blacks, and even trying to get something to read from a public library offered its share of frustration. Many public and school libraries limited access to their books to whites. Few southern cities provided library service for blacks at all, and those that did either restricted them to odd hours or only to poorly supplied "colored branches."

Several examples of this policy are reported in Charles S. Johnson's 1943 study on segregation:

James Arthur Baldwin (1924–1987) was an American author noted for his books on racial conflict in the United States. His two most famous works are collections of essays on race: *Notes of a Native Son* (1955) and *Nobody Knows My Name* (1961). Critics have praised Baldwin for his ability to convey to his readers the damage racial prejudice inflicts on both whites and blacks. In a 1965 debate with conservative author William F. Buckley Jr., Baldwin described what it was like to be African American.

"In the case of the American Negro, from the moment you are born every stick and stone, every face, is white. Since you have not yet seen a mirror, you suppose you are, too. It comes as a great shock around the age of 5, 6, or 7 to discover that the flag to which you have pledged allegiance, along with everybody else, has not pledged allegiance to you. It comes as a great shock to see Gary Cooper killing off the Indians and, although you are rooting for Gary Cooper, that the Indians are you.

It comes as a great shock to discover that the country which is your birthplace and to which you owe your life and identity has not, in its whole system of reality, evolved any place for you. The disaffection and the gap between people, only on the basis of their skins, begins there and accelerates throughout your whole lifetime."

James Baldwin's books on racial conflict depicted the damage that prejudices inflicted on both whites and blacks.

A Negro scholar in South Carolina, working on source materials in the state archives, was allowed to use the books called for, but in the basement. Another Negro student was permitted the freedom of an arrangement with the janitor to use books after library hours, while the cleaning was being done. In the State Library of Virginia there is a segregated table in the main reading room designated, "For Colored Readers." Municipal libraries in Richmond are controlled by a city ordinance which provides that Negro readers shall have a separate branch. In Atlanta no books housed in the central library or other white branches may be used by Negroes or the Negro branch.[30]

Strict rules of racial etiquette were forced on blacks in public places, and they also determined how blacks got from one place to another. Nowhere was this more evident than on public transportation.

To the Back of the Bus, Please

When intercity buses were first introduced in the South in the 1920s and 1930s, there was apparently no plan to provide seating space for blacks. Some bus lines accepted only white passengers; in some states it took legal action to force bus lines to accept black passengers. Only after experimenting with separate buses for each race did most lines finally just set aside the back seats of every bus for black occupancy.

In 1952 another problem arose for white-owned bus lines when long-distance buses first became equipped with a toilet. It was assumed that white passengers would not want to use the toilet after a black person had used it. Since segregation laws had not anticipated toilets on buses, it was up to southern bus drivers to devise a way to discourage black passengers from using the facilities. The system they devised was incredibly simple—and cruel. Whenever the driver observed in his

After experimenting with separate buses for blacks and whites, most bus lines just set aside the back seats for black occupancy.

rearview mirror a black person entering the toilet, he would drive the bus off the pavement and onto the rough shoulder of the road, thus jostling and terrorizing the toilet occupant until he or she came back out and sat down. The message was clear: Blacks were not to use the same toilet whites used on the bus.

Blacks encountered segregated facilities not only while riding a bus but also while waiting for a bus. Bus stations provided separate, but hardly equal, facilities for their black passengers. In his landmark study on segregation, Johnson reports,

> In Cleveland, Mississippi, the bus stops at a filling station where a small, comfortable waiting room is provided for white passengers, while for Negroes there is a bench in a small, poorly ventilated room which is also used as a storeroom for soft drink cases, beer cases, and tires. For white passengers clean rest rooms (one for men and one for women) are accessible from the waiting room. A single toilet for Negroes is located in the rear of the building and is not accessible from the waiting room.[31]

Riding the Rails

Another form of public transportation, the railroads, provided southern whites further opportunities to discriminate against blacks. In the first half of the twentieth century, southern trains having three or more cars usually designated one car for black passengers. On trains containing coaches, sleeping cars, club cars, or dining cars, the coach immediately behind the baggage and mail cars was usually set aside for blacks. These cars were located farther back on the train and, therefore, were less desirable because of the

cinders and smoke that blew in through the windows from the coal-burning locomotive. The Jim Crow cars were almost invariably older, less well equipped, and frequently dirty.

Railroad dining cars in the segregated South traditionally served both races but were equipped with a cloth screen that could be drawn around two tables at one end of the car. Many whites felt that such a screen was necessary to shield any nonwhite diners from the view of whites. The aversion of some white southerners to dining in view of blacks could be extreme. In some cases, white passengers even became nauseated unless the curtain was drawn.

When a black passenger riding on a train arrived at his or her destination, Jim Crow was waiting there as well. The quality and availability of facilities at railroad stations and terminals, like those at bus stations, varied widely in the South. Waiting rooms and toilets for blacks were always separate from those reserved for whites, and except in a few instances, equipment in areas reserved for blacks was older and in worse repair. The typical station had its black waiting room adjoining the baggage room, with a small window connecting it to the ticket agent's office. Blacks were served at the window only when they could get the attention of the ticket agent. The entrance to the black section was generally on the side or back of the station.

The Most Segregated Hour of the Week

Whether trying to enjoy a public park, eat in a restaurant, buy some clothes, or travel from one place to another, blacks faced constant humiliation and scorn at the hands of whites. Even many southern churches failed to provide a respite from Jim Crow. Regardless of the sermons preached inside—promising God's love for all humankind—churches were strictly segregated. To this day, southern churches remain some of the most segregated places in society. During the Jim Crow years, white churches did not welcome blacks, and some went to great lengths to prevent any Sunday morning contact between the races.

The extent to which the segregationists would go regarding worship was perhaps best illustrated by the following story, quoted in Senator Jacob Javits's 1960 study *Discrimination, U.S.A.*:

It seems that a Negro started to enter one of the largest churches in a southern city when he was stopped by a policeman at the door. The policeman said: "You can't go in here. Don't you know this is a white church?" The Negro replied: "Oh, that's all right. I'm the janitor." The officer considered this reply for a moment, then said: "Well, all right. But you better be sure. Don't let me catch you praying while you're in there!"[32]

A Strong Sense of Community

Amidst all the frustration and heartache of trying to cope with white society, black churches did provide a welcome respite. In their own churches, blacks developed a strong sense of community and family, a source of moral support that was badly needed. Within the black churches, leaders arose who served as role models for the youth and provided aid for the underprivileged. Despite widespread discrimination, or possibly because of it, blacks developed strong bonds that allowed many to prosper.

The black church played an important role in unifying black families and supporting black parents as they tried to counter the degrading influence that segregation had on their children.

Clifton L. Taulbert writes of his childhood in Glen Allan, Mississippi:

Our lives centered around the colored church. It provided the framework for civic involvement, the backdrop for leadership, a safe place for social gatherings, where our babies were blessed, our families married and our dead respected. Yes, the colored church became the sanctuary for our dreams and the closet for our secrets, and even the funerals were representative of all we were, and what we hoped to become.[33]

While fulfilling its role as a spiritual agency, the black church took on broader responsibilities. It served as a traditional community center and unifying institution in the black neighborhood. The church often served as school, lecture hall, social and recreational center, and meeting place.

But perhaps most of all, as African American Benjamin Mays recalls of the church he attended in rural South Carolina, "This was the one place where the Negroes in my community could be free and relax from the toil and oppression of the week. Among themselves they were free to show off and feel important."[34] Being able to worship in their own church and listen to their own minister not only helped nurture their dreams of freedom but also allowed them to enjoy their own version of Christian worship.

On the Road

At home in their own neighborhood and in their own church, blacks could feel at least a

Black churches helped blacks develop a sense of community and family by serving as schools, lecture halls, social and recreational centers, as well as meeting places.

small sense of security. On the road, however, that sense of security quickly evaporated. A black traveler who required overnight lodging had a hard time finding accommodations. No blacks were allowed to stay in any hotel in the South frequented by whites. As a rule, there were no hotels for blacks in small towns, but those seeking lodging might find a black-run boardinghouse where rooms were available. In the cities there were usually several small hotels reserved for blacks, but the quality was usually low and the surrounding neighborhoods could be unsafe. Most who traveled in the South stayed overnight in private homes.

Segregated lodging presented problems for integrated organizations wishing to hold conventions in the South. For example, in 1937, when the National Education Association, whose membership at the time included several hundred black teachers, met in New Orleans, the headquarters hotel objected to black convention delegates' using the formal entrance of the hotel. The management also objected to them passing through the hotel lobby on their way to convention sessions. As their solution to the "problem," the hotel proposed a temporary ladder or stair through a side window. The black members objected, and only a few attended.

On the rare occasions when the Biltmore Hotel in Atlanta, Georgia, permitted an interracial conference to be held in its meeting rooms, it refused to serve meals to black delegates, even in the privacy of the conference rooms. Consequently, the black delegates had to bring their lunches with them or make a long trek to the section of the city where blacks could obtain meals.

Inconvenience, humiliation, and uncertainty nearly always accompanied black travelers. Whether driving in a car, walking down the street, or riding on public transportation (trains and buses), blacks in the Jim Crow era experienced discrimination and, at times, open threats.

Behind the Wheel

With the age of the automobile, new situations arose where blacks came into contact with whites. Even on the road and behind the wheel, blacks had to abide by certain rules of conduct. Black motorists could apparently buy gasoline wherever it was sold, even in the Deep South, but few service stations maintained "colored" rest rooms, and those that did made no effort to keep them clean.

Early in the automobile age, whites in some communities arbitrarily denied black motorists access to public streets. As historian Neil R. McMillen writes,

> [For] a time following World War I, [in Mississippi] Jackson's Capitol Street, portions of Greenwood, the entire city of Laurel, and doubtless all or parts of many other communities were known to be open only to white motor traffic. In the Delta, custom forbade black drivers to overtake vehicles driven by whites on unpaved roads. "It's against the law for a Negro to pass a white man," a black Holmes Countian reported in 1940, "because the black man might stir up dust that would get on the white folks."[35]

Many towns also informally prohibited blacks from parking along their main roads.

In most states, the taboo against whites and nonwhites sitting together even applied to seating in automobiles. Most white drivers insisted that nonwhite passengers sit in the back seat of the car. If the car had no back seat, some would insist that the black passenger ride on the bumper or fender. Many southern whites went to these extremes rather than allow a black person to sit beside them. This was also true of some white truck drivers, even when their coworkers were black. They would insist that blacks ride in the back of their open truck in hot or cold weather—even in the rain—rather than permit them to sit in the cab.

Roadside Risks

Because they were often deprived of public transportation and were unable to afford cars of their own, many blacks could only get where they were going on foot. Walking along roadsides presented its own risks, however. In cities and towns across the South, nonwhite pedestrians knew they had better leap for the curb just as soon as the light changed because many waiting white motorists delighted in the "sport" of chasing blacks onto the curbs with their cars.

At times, being a black pedestrian was more than a little dangerous. In addition to dodging white motorists at intersections and traffic lights, walking along a southern road could be hazardous to a black person's health; many young southern teenage boys, buoyed by alcohol and the cheers and dares of their friends, delighted in terrorizing and inflicting pain and humiliation on black pedestrians.

The white South segregated the races by law and enforced custom in practically every conceivable situation in which whites and blacks might come into social contact. In addition to public transportation and public parks, blacks and whites were kept separate in hospitals, asylums, orphanages, and homes for the aged and disabled.

The Sick and the Dead

The general pattern of segregation in hospitals required the isolation of black patients from contact with white patients and, as much as possible, from contact with equipment used for whites. Private hospitals either refused to admit blacks, gave them only emergency treatment, or segregated them. Contact between black and white patients was avoided by admitting blacks through side or back doors and, in some cases, requiring them to use freight elevators. Laws or custom also required that black and white nurses tend only to the sick of their own race. Blacks who were seriously injured in automobile accidents near small southern towns were, in many instances, refused even emergency treatment at the local hospital.

Rigid segregation was also enforced in taking care of the dead. Separate black and white funeral homes existed in all parts of the South, and in many other parts of the country as well. Just as Jim Crow laws decreed that black babies had to come into the world in

Dr. Charles Richard Drew, Pioneer in Blood

Charles Drew, who was born in Washington, D.C., in 1904, became a world-renowned physician. During World War II Drew perfected the technique for separating blood plasma from whole blood so it could be used more readily in the field to save lives. Blood plasma could be given to anyone without having to be matched to a particular donor. His process saved countless lives during wartime and led to the establishment of blood banks.

At the age of forty-five, Dr. Drew was injured in an automobile accident in North Carolina on April 1, 1950. He died of loss of blood because the local hospital refused to give him a blood transfusion. The hospital was for whites only. Dr. Charles Drew was black.

separate hospitals, blacks also had to occupy separate facilities at the end of their lives. An exception to the strict separation of this intimate personal service occurred, for example, when a beloved lifelong black employee of a white family died. At the family's request, the deceased could be prepared by a white mortician and buried in a white cemetery.

The reverse, in which a black mortician handled a white body, almost never occurred and was prohibited by health codes in many states. According to one historian, an embarrassing situation took place in one southern state "when police unwittingly turned over to a Negro mortician the body of a white criminal who had blackened his face as a disguise."[36]

Cemeteries were also strictly segregated. White cemeteries usually occupied honored locations near southern towns. Many had paved drives, beautiful landscaping, expensive statuary, and perhaps even paid attendants on duty around the clock. Black cemeteries, on the other hand, were usually located next to black churches. They seldom had much in the way of ornamentation, other than what the families of the deceased furnished. In many cases, poor rural blacks simply buried their own dead under a tree near their homes.

This type of racial segregation was commonly accepted by members of both races. There were extreme measures taken in some cases, however. In some instances black bodies, buried in the mid–nineteenth century in white cemeteries with the families they had served, were relocated during the Jim Crow era to black cemeteries. Also, in Washington, D.C., a cemetery for pets at one time refused to inter the remains of pets that had belonged to black people.

The ways in which Jim Crow affected the ritual of death could become bizarre. Accord-

Leaders such as Martin Luther King Jr. expressed the demoralizing effects of segregation and fought for equality for blacks.

ing to Leon F. Litwack's *Trouble in Mind*, "Will Mathis, a convicted white felon, appealed to a judge that he be hanged at a different hour than Orlando Lester, a black man, and from a different set of gallows."[37] The request was granted.

Jim Crow's Legacy

Separate facilities? Yes. Equal? Hardly. Blacks received one message from whites, which was clearly stated and implied through treatment: Blacks were inferior to whites and would never be considered equals, law or no law.

The burden of segregation weighed on America's black population not only through legal separation from whites in public places and discrimination in business dealings but also in the general attitude most southern whites held toward blacks and the social customs with which blacks were forced to comply.

So it was that Jim Crow laws and practices affected a black person from cradle to grave. When asked in 1963 why blacks in the United States could not just wait for race relations to get better on their own, Martin Luther King Jr. eloquently expressed segregation's demoralizing effect on a particularly vulnerable group, black children:

Perhaps it is easy for those who have not felt the stinging darts of segregation to say, "Wait." But . . . when you suddenly find your tongue twisted and your speech stammering as you seek to explain to your six-year-old daughter why she can't go to the public amusement park that has just been advertised on television, and see tears welling up in her eyes when she is told that Funtown is closed to colored children, and see ominous clouds of inferiority beginning to form in her little mental sky, and see her beginning to distort her personality by developing an unconscious bitterness toward white people; when you have to concoct an answer for a five-year-old son who is asking: "Daddy, why do white people treat colored people so mean?" . . . then you will understand why we find it difficult to wait.[38]

Jim Crow's effect on children, King believed, was ultimately the most damaging, and nowhere was it more evident than in the so-called separate-but-equal southern school systems. There, attitudes and self-images created by blacks' experiences with whites became quite apparent.

3 Jim Crow Schools

Segregation of black students from white students in public schools, colleges, and universities was ordered with the provision that facilities be "separate but equal." Although whites grudgingly agreed to education for blacks, they felt strongly, particularly in the South, that allowing their children to sit in the same classrooms with black children would somehow damage them. After Reconstruction, and especially after the 1896 *Plessy v. Ferguson* Supreme Court ruling, every effort was made to keep blacks and whites apart in schools.

In public schools, segregation remained complete and unbroken throughout the South, although it extended into other states as well. During the Jim Crow years, segregation was required by law in the schools of seventeen states, concentrated in the South and the Southwest, and in the District of Columbia. It was permitted by local option in four states, and prohibited by law in only sixteen. The remaining states had no laws on the subject.

Florida, Oklahoma, Kansas, Tennessee, and other states passed laws making it illegal for white and black children to attend the same schools. They promised fines or imprisonment for anyone who dared break the law. In Kansas, the law extended to private schools as well. Georgia law accomplished its goal by stating that "no teacher receiving or teaching white and colored pupils in the same school shall be allowed any compensation at all out of the common funds."[39] In other words, one might teach an integrated class but could not expect to be paid for doing so.

Some states went to extremes to keep education of the races as separate as possible. For example, a Texas law requiring school officials to keep a census of all children living in their district even required that the names of white and black children be kept on separate lists. In 1940 Mississippi law required that textbooks provided by the state for white and black students be kept in separate warehouses. Furthermore, black and white applicants for teaching licenses were required by law to take their examinations in separate rooms.

According to the *Plessy* ruling, the facilities for the education of black children were supposed to be equal to those provided for white children. However, the buildings, supplies, teachers, and opportunities afforded black students were never even close to equal.

Racial Attitudes

Although white authorities claimed to believe that black schools were equal to those attended by whites, the fact was that some did not believe that blacks should be educated at all. In 1899 James K. Vardaman, who later served as governor of Mississippi, was quoted in *Commonwealth*, the newspaper of Greenwood, Mississippi:

In educating the Negro we implant in him all manner of aspirations and ambitions which we then refuse to allow him to gratify. It would be impossible for a Negro in Mississippi to be elected as much as a Justice of the Peace. . . . Yet people talk about elevating the race by education! It is not only folly, but it comes pretty nearly being criminal folly. The Negro isn't permitted to advance and their education only spoils a good field hand and makes a shyster lawyer or a fourth-rate teacher. It is money thrown away.[40]

This attitude flourished throughout the South, resulting not only in the complete separation of white students and teachers from their black counterparts but also in the custom of decidedly inferior instruction and opportunity for black students. In spite of these obstacles, however, some blacks struggled through the black educational system and became doctors, lawyers, and teachers. But the majority of blacks experienced an educational system designed by whites to keep them in the fields and in the kitchens.

Civil rights activist Fannie Lou Hamer's biographer, Kay Mills, recalls what a typical year of "schooling" was like as she was growing up in the Delta region of Mississippi:

Black children . . . could not aspire to much schooling, especially the boys, who had to help [with the plowing] in the spring. School for black children in the Mississippi Delta started in December, once the cotton was in, and ran through March. Often children didn't have warm clothes or shoes, so they couldn't attend classes. School would let out until the cotton was planted and the initial weeding done. Then followed two summer months of school, with children sitting in stifling classrooms in Mississippi's humid heat. Often no schools existed for black chil-

dren, and classes were conducted in tenant farmers' cabins, stores, churches, or other private buildings. . . . As late as 1950 . . . there were no four-year black high schools, . . . no publicly owned black school buildings, and . . . [according to the Bureau of Educational Research at the University of Mississippi,] "the colored schools . . . as they now exist, are in deplorable condition."[41]

Black Schools in the Rural South

The schools blacks attended, especially in the rural South, looked very much alike. Few rural black pupils will ever forget the conditions under which they tried to learn, even as late as the 1950s. They sat in run-down, primitive, one-room wooden structures with unsteady floors, cracks in the walls and roof, and a potbellied, wood-burning stove in the center of the room. They sat on rough backless benches made of split logs. The only light in the room came through small glassless windows. Any furnishings in the room had to be scrounged from dumps or trash piles in the neighborhood or made from scrap lumber by students' fathers.

Black schools in urban areas were not much better. If a school building was furnished by the local school board, it was most often a run-down building no one else wanted. Its equipment was invariably cast-off from the white school, if provided at all. Makeshift blackboards might be available, but teachers were asked to furnish their own chalk and eraser.

According to Leon F. Litwack, southern black schools not only had to contend with substandard, often unpainted buildings, they also did not receive even the simplest supplies:

Most rural black children attended classes in one-room schoolhouses, sat on backless benches, and read by light that entered through a small glassless window.

In the absence of the most basic school supplies and furnishings, teachers and students improvised as best they could. A baseball "did duty" in one schoolroom to explain to students the motions of the earth; sand spread on the floor served as a relief map for geography classes; and pebbles retrieved from the school grounds were used as "the basis of a talk on common sense."[42]

Another black southerner, while reminiscing with his son about conditions at his rural separate-but-equal school in the 1940s, reported that when black students got their few textbooks, which were always well used, they would look inside the cover to see whose names were there. The names would always belong to white children. He recalled,

We always got the old books, the white kids got 'em first. And there'd always be pages missing, where if you read two chapters relative to something, you couldn't finish. If the third chapter completed the subject matter, then that chapter would be deliberately cut out, or the pages torn up, and you'd never know how it finished. . . . I think it was to keep us from doing enough work to get a high school diploma.[43]

History Lessons

The content of the textbooks, as well as their physical condition, served to keep blacks subservient. The history lessons to which black students were exposed in the few textbooks they received reinforced the concept of white superiority—of Anglo-Saxon institutions and the "white ways" of thinking and acting. Their books taught essentially a sanitized history of Anglo-Saxons and northern Europeans: brave Pilgrims, devout Puritans, and infallible founding fathers.

Not only were the conditions of black schools deplorable, but they received used textbooks that had pages missing and had inadequate or nonexistent visual aids.

The history they learned was not black history, nor did it have much to do with their lives or with the lives of their parents or their neighbors. What little they learned of their own history was invariably a stereotyped image of black people as the least civilized of the races. They were portrayed as irresponsible, thoughtless, foolish, childlike people who seemed pleased with their low position in American life. Civil rights activist Fannie Lou Hamer recalled the way blacks were portrayed in the textbooks she and her classmates were provided with in the 1920s:

> When I was in public school, the state of Mississippi was responsible for doing a very sad thing. When I was in school—it must have been in a child's third reader—I read about a little child and this little child was black and his name was Epamonandus. First place, it was stupid to put a word that big in a book for a kid. Second place, it was a disgrace the way they had this little child and the things that he was doing.[44]

According to Hamer, the child was portrayed as stupid, as were his mother and his grandmother.

The history black children read was one in which black people gladly submitted to the will of whites and served them willingly and faithfully. "Saved" from the darkness of heathen Africa and brought to the "civilized" world, grateful slaves found contentment and happiness. According to historian Litwack,

> Illustrations of blacks, if they appeared at all, depicted well-fed, carefree laborers frolicking in the fields; amiable, deferential Uncle Toms greeting their patronizing and loving masters, hat in hand, evincing a demeanor of contentment, docility, and faithfulness.[45]

Lunchtime

School lunches, like adequate textbooks, were almost always provided at white schools but seldom at black ones. Author Clifton L. Taulbert recalls that his parents and grandparents had attended an old plantation school, set up just after Reconstruction. At those poor schools, sharecropping parents took turns providing a cheap, simple hot lunch for all the children. Each day would bring a variation of beans, peas, and cornbread, or peas, okra, beans, and cornbread.

Taulbert describes how the meal was prepared each day:

> The ladies would get permission to leave the fields a little early and while [the teacher] was teaching, they'd be getting the old iron stove hot. These field hands—

White school children were almost always provided with buses, school lunches, and adequate textbooks.

turned-volunteer-cooks would heat the beans on the stove and turn one of the long church benches into a table to serve the hot meal.[46]

As his parents told him, the meals were plain but hot and tasty and certainly better than nothing, which was what they could expect from white school districts.

Those Big Yellow School Buses

Not only did black students have to contend with run-down buildings, inadequate supplies, and volunteer lunches provided by their parents, even getting to school proved to be a hardship for many. Buses, usually provided for rural whites, were seldom, if ever, provided for blacks. A black student's chances of getting to ride to school on a free school bus were one-third those of a white student's. Many who grew up in rural areas of the South reported walking miles every day to attend school. As they walked down dirt roads on their way to school, black students were often passed by shiny new school buses full of white students. As one black parent remembers,

In those days black kids didn't ride the bus, we walked, sometimes miles. The white kids did get to ride, and the reason

Controversial Children's Books

When the Supreme Court decided in 1954 to desegregate U.S. public schools, many southern whites reacted desperately. They frantically searched local libraries for books that were thought to be pro-integration. The book hunt began in June 1959 with the attack on an illustrated children's story *The Rabbit's Wedding* by Garth Williams. The story described a white rabbit and a black rabbit who lived and played in a large forest. The black rabbit wanted to marry the white rabbit. In the story, all the other little rabbits came out to see how happy they both were, they danced all night in the moonlight, were wed, and lived together happily in the forest.

Alabama's Senator E. O. Eddins promptly demanded that the book be taken off the shelves and burned. In the Orlando, Florida, *Sentinel*, columnist Henry Balch wrote at the time: "As soon as you pick up the book you realize these rabbits are integrated. One of the techniques of brainwashing is conditioning minds to accept what the brainwashers want accepted."

The controversy over this book made front-page news and reached international proportions. It led to other books' being thrown out of southern libraries and destroyed. *The Three Little Pigs* was chosen because one of the illustrated animals was a black pig. Another book, *The First Book of Fishing*, was attacked in the Shreve Memorial Library in Shreveport, Louisiana, because it had illustrations of black and white children fishing and picnicking together. A fourth, *Two Is a Team*, was attacked by the grand dragon of the Alabama Ku Klux Klan, Robert M. Shelton. The book tells the story of a black boy named Ted and a white boy named Paul who are playmates. The book is illustrated in color and shows the two children visiting in each other's homes and playing with children of other races.

we knew it was because they'd ride past us on their buses and insult us, or yell something racist and laugh, and you'd be there out in the rain.[47]

Teacher Training

Once a black student struggled over the miles of dirt roads to get to school, he or she would oftentimes be taught by someone who had never been to college and who might not have even been to high school. The educational preparation of a black teacher varied considerably from state to state and between urban and rural areas. In much of the rural South, black teachers were not educated past the seventh or eighth grades. William Holtzclaw, who grew up in Alabama and later taught in Mississippi, recalls that "when a pupil got as far as the word 'abasement' in the Webster blue-back speller, he or she was made an assistant teacher and shortly thereafter relieved the white teachers."[48]

Most black parents felt that allowing ill-prepared teachers into black classrooms was designed to further prevent their children from getting a good education. In their minds, the philosophy behind this practice was consistent with white people's fears of the effects of black learning. One historian writes,

[Some] whites, fearing the consequences of overeducated blacks, chose to encourage blacks to enter teaching without becoming scholars. That is, authorities framed examinations that black applicants could easily pass without a high school education. In Beaufort County, South Carolina, a [white] teacher complained that a number of black graduates had failed to pass the qualifying examination and suggested that the questions be

made simpler. Agreeing with her suggestion, the white superintendent drew up a list of questions—"too trifling to bear the name," one resident wrote—with the word "Negroes" at the top, while preparing a different and more demanding qualifying examination for whites. Protesting this double standard, a black teacher warned against permitting whites "with their feigned sympathy" to enlist her people in a scheme calculated to promote ignorance.[49]

White Fears

It is not surprising that whites in the Jim Crow South considered it vital that black men and women not be allowed to acquire even the barest essentials of learning. According to one historian,

Knowledge encouraged independence and free thought. Knowledge opened up new vistas, introduced people to a larger world than the local town and county. Knowledge permitted workers to calculate their earnings and expenditures. These were sufficient incentives for whites to maintain black illiteracy—or to place clear limits on how much knowledge blacks should acquire and to make certain it was the right kind of knowledge imparted by the right kind of teachers.[50]

Explanations offered by whites as the basis for segregation in public institutions were reported in Charles S. Johnson's 1943 study on segregation:

Physical and racial aversion, uncleanliness, criminality, lack of morals, and ineducability. The beliefs that Negro children would contaminate white children and that the mental difference requires separate treatment are frequently held. A school official said that the colored child's mind was always two years behind that of the white.[51]

A railroad mechanic in Georgia, who did not think education would be either possible or useful to a black man, once remarked, "He's got a thick head, he can't get further. A little education is a poor thing, and that's all the further the average nigger gets, and that ruins him."[52]

Burdens of the System

Whatever reasons whites gave for maintaining segregated schools, the effects of such a system on blacks has been clearly documented. Official U.S. government figures have shown that throughout the decades of Jim Crow gross discrepancies existed between white and black educational facilities in states segregated by law. In the 1940s, for example, the value of school property accessible to blacks was less than one-fourth of what it was to whites. The annual per capita (per person) expenditure by states on black schooling was only one-half what it was for whites. Black classrooms, overcrowded in any case, contained, on the average, a dozen students more than white classrooms in similar areas.

Functional illiteracy was three times more prevalent among young southern blacks than among young southern whites during the 1940s. Because of differences in the quality of instruction offered in the South, a black student might not learn as much in six years as a white child learned in three. Black children who succeeded in getting more than six years of schooling would be offered only such

Black Self-Image

Young blacks in the age of Jim Crow were constantly reminded of their inferior status in American society. Leon F. Litwack, in his book *Trouble in Mind*, quotes Albon Holsey, a black man who grew up in the first decade of the twentieth century. Even as a teenager, Holsey knew that the odds were stacked against him, no matter what he did.

"At fifteen, I was fully conscious of the racial difference, and while I was sullen and resentful in my soul, I was beaten and knew it. I knew then that I could never aspire to be President of the United States, nor Governor of my State, nor mayor of my city; I knew that the front doors of white homes in my town were not for me to enter, except as a servant; I knew that I could only sit in the peanut gallery at our theatre, and could only ride on the back seat of the electric car and in the Jim Crow car on the train. I had bumped into the color line and knew that so far as white people were concerned, I was just another nigger."

vocational courses as bricklaying, carpentry, and sewing. White children pursuing vocational goals would be given the chance to study for higher-paying, more technical occupations such as aviation, printing, or cosmetology.

Higher Education

Segregation during the Jim Crow years kept black students out of institutions of higher education, preventing them from getting the education they needed to secure good-paying jobs and positions of influence in the community. In the 1940s, blacks who wanted to become lawyers, for example, had only half a dozen law schools in the nation from which to choose. The others were for whites only.

Beginning in the forties, though, blacks began challenging segregated states in the courts, demanding equal access to university courses, particularly in their law schools. Most states resisted such challenges, but some tried to sidestep the issue by hastily constructing what they considered "equal" facilities for black law students.

When, in 1946, the courts ordered the state of Texas to admit Herman Marion Sweatt, a black man, to the University of Texas law school, it instead quickly erected a three-room law school at a Texas college for blacks. South Carolina tried to establish a one-room law school at a state-supported black college in 1947 after a federal judge ordered the state to admit black war veteran John H. Wrighten to the University of South Carolina law school. That same year, the U.S. Supreme Court ordered Oklahoma to provide equal opportunity for the study of law to Ada Lois Sipuel, and that state's remedy, too, was a one-room law school at a black college.

Even when black students attended college, they encountered inferior facilities and instruction. In the segregated South of the 1940s, the ratio of public and private expenditures for white colleges as compared to black ones ranged from forty-two to one in Kentucky to three to one in Washington, D.C. Of the approximately four thousand doctorate degrees issued annually in the United States during that decade, only eight went each year to African American graduates.

It was similarly difficult to receive training in other professions. Despite a real need for more black physicians, for example, blacks found it extremely difficult to get training in this field. Of the 77 medical colleges in the United States in the 1940s, 20 were located in the South and would not accept black students. The situation outside the South was little better; of the remaining 57 schools nationwide, only 19 would admit blacks. Out of approximately six hundred black medical students enrolled nationwide at one point during the Jim Crow era, fewer than one hundred were in white medical colleges. Blacks wanting to be nurses also faced difficulty. Of the 1,280 nursing schools in the United States during the forties, 1,214 were open to whites only.

Black Attitudes Leading to Change

If students, parents, and teachers accepted a separate-and-unequal school system, that acceptance was seldom voluntary and it did not necessarily imply that blacks were satisfied with the system as it existed. As early as 1918, a group of black parents and concerned black citizens appealed to the all-white Mississippi state legislature asking for racial fairness in education. Their words echoed the feelings of many:

> We cannot understand by what process of reasoning that you can conclude that [it] is humane, just, or reasonable to take the common funds of all and use it to the glory of your children and leave ours in ignorance, squalor and shame. The Negro has been silent, gentlemen, but not asleep to these gross neglects, for these facts are too patent [obvious], even to the most obtuse [slow to understand].[53]

Obtuse or not, segregation and favoritism toward whites in every aspect of education

Trouble at Central High—the Black Point of View

The school board in Little Rock, Arkansas, decided to begin desegregation at the high school level in the fall of 1957, three years after the U.S. Supreme Court ordered school desegregation. It planned to introduce a handpicked group of nine black students into previously all-white Central High School. On Wednesday, September 4, the nine black teenagers attempted to enter Central High, which, by that time, was surrounded by National Guard troops and an angry segregationist mob. Eight of the black students were accompanied by city police and a group of concerned adults. One of the black students, however, fifteen-year-old Elizabeth Eckford, had somehow not been notified of the group's plans and approached the school alone.

In *Growing Up Southern*, Eckford recalls that she got off the city bus a block from the school and saw a large crowd of people standing across the street from soldiers guarding the high school. As she walked toward the school, the crowd suddenly got very quiet. For a moment all she could hear was the shuffling of their feet. Then someone shouted, "Here she comes, get ready!" She moved away from the crowd on the sidewalk and into the street.

The crowd moved in closer and followed, calling her names. She said she was not afraid, just a little nervous. She writes, "Then my knees started to shake all of a sudden and I wondered whether I could make it to the center entrance a block away. It was the longest block I ever walked in my whole life."

When the guards at the main entrance would not let her pass, she turned to face the angry crowd. They moved closer, and someone yelled, "Lynch her! Lynch her!"

"I tried to see a friendly face somewhere in the mob—someone who maybe would help. I looked into the face of an old woman and it seemed a kind face, but when I looked at her again, she spat on me.

Then I looked down the block and saw a bench at the bus stop. I thought, 'If I can only get there I will be safe.'

When I finally got there, I don't think I could have gone another step. I sat down and the mob crowded up and began shouting all over again. Someone hollered, 'Drag her over to this tree! Let's take care of that nigger.' Just then a white man sat down beside me, put his arm around me, and patted my shoulder. He raised my chin and said, 'Don't let them see you cry.'"

Three years after the U.S. Supreme Court ordered the desegregation of schools, Little Rock's Central High handpicked nine black teens to enter the school.

One of the white students taunting Elizabeth Eckford at Little Rock's Central High School on that day in the fall of 1957 was Anne Thompson. She, like most southerners, felt segregation was simply the way of life. She had never known anything else. As in most southern cities, blacks lived in one part of town and whites in another.

She is quoted in the 1998 book *The Century*, written by ABC newsman Peter Jennings and Todd Brewster.

"I was a fifteen-year-old tenth grader when they made the announcement. At first many of the parents refused to believe that it was actually going to happen. Some parents formed groups and committees to try and stop it, but my parents didn't really take part in any of that. It's not that they weren't interested; they just didn't know what to do, or where to go. Ultimately, they just decided that their child was not going to an integrated school, and that was that. I don't think it was really out of hate for anyone. I think it was out of ignorance and fear of the unknown.

I honestly can't remember exactly when I first saw Elizabeth Eckford. . . . All of a sudden Elizabeth was walking down the sidewalk and there was this rush. We had to let her know that she couldn't come to our school. So we ran up behind her and started chanting and jeering, 'Two-four-six-eight. We don't want to integrate!' And, 'Go back to your own school!'

Throughout it all, Elizabeth was absolutely stoic. You couldn't tell that she heard anything. She held her head slightly downward and just walked. Even as I was jeering, I couldn't help but feel sorry for her. I realized then that this must all be very hard for her. I don't know that I felt empathy, because I don't know that I could really feel what she was feeling. But I did feel sorry for her, and I was saddened. That day when the black students entered the white school, we felt as if they beat us. They won; we lost."

continued until halfway through the twentieth century. At that point, blacks pushed whites to integrate schools in the South. In 1954 the Supreme Court finally overruled *Plessy v. Ferguson* in the case of *Brown v. Board of Education* and ordered all public schools desegregated. Lawyers for the National Association for the Advancement of Colored People (NAACP) argued the case before the Court.

Central to the NAACP's argument was the belief that segregated schools injured black children—permanently scarring them with a sense of inferiority. Included in their legal presentation was the following report by psychologist Kenneth Clark. Clark had tested sixteen black children in Clarendon County, South Carolina, to determine how they felt about themselves. The children were shown a white doll and a black doll and were given the following instructions:

1. Give me the doll that you like best.
2. Give me the doll that is the nice doll.
3. Give me the doll that looks bad.
4. Give me the doll that is a nice color.
5. Give me the doll that is most like you.

The children's responses to the questions graphically illustrated how they felt about being black. According to Clark,

Some of the children reacted with such intense emotion to the "dolls test" that they were unable to continue. One little girl who had shown a clear preference for the white doll and who described the brown doll as "ugly" and "dirty" broke into a torrent of tears when she was asked to identify herself with one of the dolls. . . . These children saw themselves as inferior, and they accepted the inferiority as part of reality. . . . Segregation is the way in which a society tells a group of human beings that they are inferior to other groups of human beings in society. It really is internalized in children. . . . It influences the child's view of himself.[54]

White Resistance to Change

Throughout the South in the 1950s, white segregationists disagreed with the Court's ruling, demanding that their states resist it. Between 1957 and 1959, a sense of desperation on their part brought a fever of rebellion and a nagging fear to the South. Books supporting school desegregation were banned and library shelves purged. Slanted articles and editorials opposed to the high court's ruling appeared in local newspapers. National magazines that reported on desegregation or racial equality, including *Time* and *Life*, were considered anti-South and disappeared from southern newsstands.

Television programs and films portraying blacks as equals were also withheld from the southern public. Teachers, preachers, and college professors were questioned—harassed—and, if any supported equality of the races and integration of the schools, they were driven from their professions or fled the South.

The results of the South's resistance to desegregation were bloodshed and violence, hatred and humiliation. Eventually, though, blacks won the right to an education equal to that of whites. With decent education came opportunity to earn a better living. That opportunity also came after much hard work to overcome the effects of Jim Crow in the workplace.

4 On the Job

Discrimination and segregation in the workplace were a way of life for blacks from just after Reconstruction until the changes brought about by the civil rights movement of the 1950s and 1960s took hold. During the Jim Crow era, only menial jobs were available to blacks; for black men in the South, that usually meant farming or janitorial work. Women were limited to working as field hands (alongside their husbands and older children) or as domestic servants in white households. In a few instances, blacks became teachers in black schools and colleges, doctors, lawyers, dentists, and businessmen, but their incomes were always lower than those of whites in the same professions partly because they were denied access to wealthier white clients and patients.

In most of the segregated South, state and/or local laws required that whenever an industry hired black workers, they would be separated from whites as much as possible. A South Carolina statute was typical:

It shall be unlawful for any person, firm, or corporation engaged in the business of cotton textile manufacturing in this state to allow or permit operatives, help and labor of different races to labor and work together within the same room, or to use the same doors of entrance and exit at the same time, or to use and occupy the same pay ticket windows or doors for paying off its operatives and laborers at the same time, or to use the same stairway and windows at the same time, or to use at any time

Discrimination in the workplace meant that only menial jobs, such as domestic service, were available for black women.

the same lavatories, toilets, drinking-water buckets, pails, cups, dippers, or glasses.[55]

Farmwork

In the rural South, from the days of Reconstruction until the age of mechanization during the 1920s through 1940s, the majority of physical labor was accomplished by black farmhands in much the same way as it had been under slavery before the Civil War. After Emancipation, blacks, by law, could not be owned by whites, but their economic dependence on white farm owners kept the vast majority of rural southern blacks in almost the same condition as when they had been slaves.

Poor blacks were either tenant farmers, renting a plot of land from a white farmer for a yearly cash payment, or sharecroppers, who farmed the white man's land for a share of the crop. In the farming system that evolved, both black tenant farmers and black sharecroppers depended on the crops they raised not only to support and feed their families but also to repay money advanced by the white landlord for operating expenses such as seed, fertilizer, and basic farm equipment.

Since the farm owner furnished almost everything necessary for growing the crop and wanted his farm laborers tied to the land, he usually arranged things so that his tenants did not earn much for a year's work. Since the tenant farmers and sharecroppers were entirely dependent on the owner of the plantation, they were compelled to do almost whatever he demanded.

Tenant Farmers

Tenant farmers made verbal agreements with the landowner sometime around the begin-

ning of the year. At that time, they agreed to a contract that was then enforced by law. Since most of the tenants were uneducated and had little or no knowledge of law, they easily gave away their rights, not knowing what they were signing. Illiterate tenants, who were unable to sign their names, usually made a mark, most often an X. Some indicated their agreement by just touching the pen.

In reality, both the black tenant farmer and the sharecropper worked the white man's land, planted his seeds, and plowed with his mules and his plow. They harvested crops owed largely to the white man in return for those seeds, that plow, and those mules, as well as for the clothes they and their families wore and the food they consumed.

In a study of black tenant farmers, social scientist Charles S. Johnson reported that on southern plantations in 1934, the usual income for a couple, if both husband and wife worked as tenants on a one-horse farm, probably averaged a cash value of only $260 a year. However, they paid about half the value of their cotton in rent, used the corn they raised to feed their livestock, and ate the potatoes, peas, and sorghum they grew along with the cotton. As a result, very little cash was handled. They managed to live on the advances received from the landowner or by borrowing money for food and clothing and permitting their crop to be taken to repay their debts.

Sharecroppers and Day Laborers

Another type of farmer, the sharecropper, farmed on the condition that he give the landlord a large percentage of his crop. If the cropper had neither tools of his own nor any form of capital, he had to borrow everything from the landowner. When he was furnished tools and work animals in addition to the land, he got only a third of the cotton raised instead of the usual half.

In addition to tenant farmers and share-croppers, some blacks served as day laborers, working for wages. In addition to their low daily wage, customarily fifty to sixty cents a day for men and forty cents for women, they might be allowed small patches of land on which to raise vegetables for their families.

Probably the lowest class of farm laborers were those who did not receive a regular salary but instead received what was known as a "hand's share" of the crops. This was just enough to keep them alive. One elderly black woman who lived alone in a one-room shack and worked for a hand's share told the following story in 1934:

> I works for a hand's share in the crop with the folks 'cross dere. My husband been dead. . . . It's mighty tight on me to have to go working in dese fields half starved, and I ain't had a bit of money to buy a piece of cloth as big as my hand since I been back. I washed fer white people in

A Tenant Farmer's "Contract"

The contracts tenant farmers were forced to sign were definitely not in their favor. In addition, interpretation of these agreements was left in the hands of the planters and plantation owners. The plight of the tenants can easily be seen in the terms of the following lease, which is excerpted from Chalmers Archer Jr.'s book, *Growing Up Black in Rural Mississippi: Memories of a Family, Heritage of a Place.*

"You the tenant . . . agree that if you violate this contract, or neglect or abandon or fail or (in Mr. _____'s [the landowner's] judgement) violate this contract or fail to properly work or till the land early or at proper times, or in case you should become disabled or legally sick or hurt while working this land or should die during the term of your lease, or fail to gather or save the crops when made, or fail to pay the rents or advances made by me [the landowner], whenever due, then in case of full possession of said premises, crops and improvements, in which event this contract may become void and canceled at my option, and all indebtedness by you for advances or rent shall at once become due and payable to me who may treat them as due and payable without further notice to you; and you hereby agree to surrender quietly and peacefully the possession of said premises to me at said time, in which event I am hereby authorized to transfer, sell or dispose of all property thereon you have any interest in, and in order to entitle me to do so, it shall not be necessary to give any notice of any failure or violation of this contract by you, the execution of this lease being sufficient notice of default on the part of you, and shall be so construed between the parties hereto, any law, usage or custom to the contrary notwithstanding."

In simplified language, the contract could have read, "I, the landowner, will determine whether or not you, the tenant, have upheld your part of the contract, and if I say you have not, I will show up at your place and legally take everything you have—and I am not required to notify you of my decision."

Because of their economic dependency on white farm owners, a majority of rural blacks were kept in the same conditions as when they were slaves.

Birmingham, and dey was good to me. I am jest gitting 'long by the hardest. I works for dese people for a hand's share of the crop. Dey gives me a load of corn and a load of potatoes. I gits some of all the other stuff what's made, and when selling cotton dey give you a little money out of the seed. I don't see no money on time. Dey gives me a little something to eat 'cause I works wid dem and dey gives me a little groceries.[56]

Southern farmworkers, whether tenant farmers, sharecroppers, or simple laborers, worked from dawn to dusk. In the 1940s, blacks who worked for wages put in twelve-hour days for two dollars. They had to be on the truck or in the field at six o'clock in the morning and didn't get off until six in the evening. Their travel time, going to and from the field, was not paid time.

Black Landowners

As hard as it was to get ahead under this system, some managed, through luck or good farming practices, to save enough money to buy their own piece of land. Even then, most faced tremendous obstacles. In 1903 the black leader, social activist, scholar, and writer W. E. B. Du Bois reported on the difficulties blacks faced when trying to purchase land in the late nineteenth century:

I have seen, in the Black Belt of Georgia, an ignorant, honest Negro buy and pay for a farm in installments three separate times, and then in the face of law and decency the enterprising American who sold it to him pocketed the money and deed and left the black man landless, to labor on his own land at thirty cents a day. I have seen a black farmer fall in debt to a white storekeeper, and that storekeeper go to his farm and strip it of every single marketable article—mules, ploughs [plows], stored crops, tools, furniture, bedding, clocks, looking-glass [mirror]—and all this without a sheriff or officer, in the face of the law for homestead exemptions, and without rendering to a single responsible person any account or reckoning.[57]

W. E. B. Du Bois was a black leader, social activist, scholar, and writer who reported on the difficulties blacks faced under Jim Crow laws.

Off the Farm

Outside the farm belt, blacks likewise faced hardships trying to make a living in the white man's world. Martin Luther King Jr. tried to explain to white Americans just what blacks had to face on the job and what they had come to expect under the Jim Crow laws:

> If you wanted a job . . . you had better settle on doing menial work as a porter or laborer. If you were fortunate enough to get a job, you could expect that promotions to a better status or more pay would come, not to you, but to a white employee regardless of your comparative talents. On your job, you would eat in a separate place and use a water fountain and lavatory labeled "Colored" in conformity to citywide ordinances.[58]

White Jobs vs. Black Jobs

Because of the limited education provided by black schools, many black applicants were less qualified for jobs that required specific skills. Thus, employers who did not want to hire blacks found it easy to refuse to hire them by claiming their decision was based solely on the applicant's abilities. In actuality, many white employers simply did not want blacks working alongside their white employees. To assure an all-white workplace, most job applications included questions about race and many times required a picture of the applicant to help employers identify nonwhite applicants. As long as schools were segregated, the workplace reflected that segregation, perpetuating enforced inferiority of black workers to white workers.

Unskilled jobs were therefore given to blacks while whites worked in positions of authority. Eventually jobs became classified as "white jobs" as opposed to "nigger work." Blacks worked with their hands while whites worked as their bosses. Occasionally poor white workers, because of a lack of education, ended up with jobs usually given to blacks. When this occurred, they could find themselves as social outcasts among other whites.

The black person's place in the occupational structure of the Jim Crow South was largely determined by racial attitudes and beliefs. A popular belief among southern whites was that a young black man could do heavy work but, according to many work supervisors, must be driven as one might an animal.

Black men were usually given unskilled jobs that required hard manual labor, while technical and clerical jobs were saved for whites.

Blacks were thus regarded as best suited for manual labor but hardly suited for technical or clerical work. An example of this racial belief is reflected in an interview with the manager of an oil company in Louisiana, which is quoted in Charles S. Johnson's 1943 study *Patterns of Negro Segregation*. In characterizing the black laborer, the manager explains,

> The Negro is like a mule; a stolid sort of creature. He plods along, does his work well at his own speed, and doesn't wear himself out like the emotional white man. The Southern nigger never worries about anything. Give him a full stomach and he's happy. I have worked all my life on the farm, and I envy him that. The Negro is too sluggish mentally for work in business. He just drifts along at a pace of his own. If you put him on a team he just lets them walk to town. Once in a while you get a good one as a mechanic on a truck, but they are the exceptions.[59]

This example was typical of the attitude held by most whites in the Jim Crow era—that blacks were incapable of anything more than physical labor. Blacks seeking alternatives to field labor in southern towns and cities usually found themselves confronted with the familiar reply, "This is white man's work," when they sought to improve their situation.

The Black Man's "Place"

Applying for a job, even one previously held by a black person, was often a humiliating experience. During his high school years in Orangeburg, South Carolina, Benjamin Mays, a young black man, applied for a house job one of his friends had recently left. When he knocked at the front door of the house and asked about the position held by his friend Mr. Kearse, Mays immediately realized he had made two big mistakes: knocking at the front door of a white person's home and referring to his black friend as "Mr." The white homeowner angrily cursed him and made it perfectly clear that no one by the name of *Mr.* Kearse had ever worked for him. "Isaiah worked here," he said, "and if you want to see me go to the back door."[60]

Once on the job, blacks sometimes found themselves working under the direction of whites who were less capable than they were. When African American Claude Walton started working for a Mississippi highway crew in 1949, he was only fourteen years old. It was his first job away from the farm:

Our job was to plant the sod and grass along the side of the highway. The black men did all the heavy work, the dirty work, planting, tamping the sod into place. We had a machine, a big heavy tool that tamped the sod into place, and you had to be strong to lift it all day. The white guys drove the trucks. They were from the Delta, and they didn't believe in calling you by your name, they'd either call you "boy" or "nigger." It didn't make them no difference. . . . They were a loud and rough bunch. It didn't seem to me like they did anything but booze and chase women and fight, and sit on the top of the truck and tell you what to do.

One day I pointed out to the foreman a place where a mistake had been made and needed fixing. . . . One of his assistants said to him, "This nigger knows everything." All I recall from the rest of that is a cold chill going through me. Why was I a "nigger" when all I was trying to

do was work hard, do a good job? That day changed me. I just wanted to make a living and not depend on anybody, not be dependent on anybody else.[61]

Black workers often found that white supervisors behaved differently when they were alone. When only one white person was present, he or she would usually treat black workers with some respect, but when three or four whites were present, they would become disrespectful. And when more than one white was present, anything bad that happened was blamed on the black workers.

The attitude that blacks were only suited to certain types of work was not limited to whites, however. Many older blacks taught their own children not to expect to be able to do everything a white person could do. As one elderly retired field hand explained to his grandson,

Niggers is built for service, like a mule, and dey needn't 'spect nothin' else. . . . A nigger's place is in de field and de road and de tunnel and de woods, wid a pick or shovel or ax or hoe or plow. God made a nigger like a mule to be close to nature and git his livin' by de sweat o' his brow like de Good Book says.[62]

Some black children were taught that they were only suited for menial jobs such as janitorial, domestic, or farmwork, and they should not aspire to anything greater. Parents who taught their children this attitude were trying to protect them from having their false hopes crushed. Most black parents knew the system was stacked against them. Worse still, years of being told they were inferior led many blacks to believe it to be true. And the arrival of modern technology and automation only served to reemphasize that idea.

Thousands of blacks were employed by the railroads until improvements in highways and the growth of the airline industry caused a decline in the demand for train travel.

Mechanization

As technology increasingly changed the nature of work in the late nineteenth and early twentieth centuries, black workers found themselves particularly affected—and for the worse. The beginnings of automation and mechanization were a curse for black labor, even though many people thought such advances were a blessing to the national economy. Since discrimination and a lack of education confined most blacks to unskilled and semiskilled labor, they were the first to suffer when a new technological development came along.

The role of blacks in the railroad industry supplies a particularly vivid example of the effects of these changes. In the nineteenth century, hundreds of thousands of blacks were employed by the railroads. Improvements in highways in the 1930s and the growth of the airline industry caused declines in business for railroads. By the 1960s fewer than 50,000 blacks worked in this area of transportation as opposed to over 350,000 years earlier. Blacks who had previously found steady work as porters, baggage handlers, and kitchen assistants found themselves without jobs. Moreover, comparable jobs in the airline industry, such as flight attendant positions, were reserved for whites.

Other industries presented similar problems. Blacks working in the coal mining, steel, and meatpacking industries were hit hardest when technological changes eliminated unskilled jobs. Moreover, when faced with a choice between firing a white employee and a black one, companies usually fired the black one first, regardless of who had held the job the longest.

Those industries that continued to rely on unskilled labor, such as construction, kept black workers out of higher-paid skilled jobs. In this effort, management was aided by the trade unions. Millions of dollars were spent each year on publicly funded building projects for which blacks paid taxes but could draw no paycheck. Martin Luther King Jr., reflecting on the construction projects erected by slave labor before the Civil War, writes:

> No one who saw the spanning bridges, the grand mansions, the sturdy docks and stout factories of the South could question the Negro's ability to build if he were given a chance for apprenticeship training. It was plain, hard, raw discrimination that shut him out of decent employment.[63]

When jobs relegated to blacks—those that had involved backbreaking labor—became attractive to whites due to advances in technology or engineering, blacks often lost those jobs to whites. Neil R. McMillen, in *Dark Journey: Black Mississippians in the Age of Jim Crow,* reports,

> In some instances, black workers were forced out as improved working conditions and white economic needs made their jobs more acceptable to the dominant race. The most notorious example involved black trainmen. . . . Although many blacks had been driven from responsible positions in the freight yards early in the [twentieth] century, a substantial number continued to work as switchmen, brakemen, and firemen, positions that until World War I were thought to be too dirty and dangerous for whites. Modernization of equipment and other innovations, however, rendered these jobs more appealing, and the clamor for black exclusion began.[64]

In many cases, blacks who refused to resign from their positions were threatened, flogged, and, in some cases, killed so that whites could take their places.

Opportunities for Blacks

Within the confines of the black community, opportunities existed for economic prosperity, professional careers, and private ownership of businesses. Many blacks owned businesses that catered to an entirely black clientele. There were successful retail merchants, barbers, hairdressers, doctors, dentists, mechanics, contractors, electricians, plumbers, bookkeepers, and restaurateurs.

Black entrepreneurs emerged in the late nineteenth and early twentieth centuries to serve an increasingly separate society, providing insurance, loans, and undertaking, all services that white businessmen or companies sometimes refused. As long as their businesses did not compete with white-owned enterprises, blacks were allowed to become as prosperous as they could. Given the limits imposed by the Jim Crow system, their successes were extraordinary.

Although Jim Crow laws governed who might be hired to work in a business, no such formal restrictions governed who might shop in stores. In the white-owned businesses of the rural South, the country store was the one universal meeting ground of the two races. Custom required social distance, however, and it was understood that physical closeness in the store did not imply social equality or intimacy. In the cities of the South the treatment of blacks in private commercial establishments was a matter of local custom, usually determined by how the manager and clerks interpreted the strength of public opinion on the subject.

Generally all business establishments fronting the town square or main street of southern towns were owned and operated by white people. Black-operated businesses were usually found on back streets or city blocks set apart for black use.

With a few exceptions in the South, banks in cities as well as small towns accepted black business. While most banks accepted deposits from African Americans, there were some that refused to make loans to them.

Black Professionals

Blacks who wanted to become professionals—doctors, lawyers, or dentists, for example—first had to face the daunting task of finding the proper training and certification. Few medical schools or law schools were available for blacks during the Jim Crow years. Of the nation's fourteen black medical colleges founded between 1868 and 1900, for instance, only two survived into the 1920s. Likewise, training for blacks in white universities was an unheard-of practice at the time. In the early years of the twentieth century, an official of the University of Georgia's medical school vowed, "There are no niggers in this school and there never have been and there never will be as long as one stone of its building remains upon another." The dean of the Hospital College of Medicine in Louisville, Kentucky, bragged that it had "never matriculated a 'coon' in all its history and never will so long as I am Dean."[65]

White professionals dominated all the important fields. They controlled judicial institutions, social welfare agencies, hospitals, and professional and business associations. Certain fields traditionally sought to exclude blacks during the age of Jim Crow—specifically architecture, chemistry, metallurgy, engineering, publishing, law, and social work. Even the

The Candy Man

In *Once upon a Time When We Were Colored*, Clifton L. Taulbert recounts his experience as a child trying to help his mother support their family in rural Mississippi. To earn extra money, Taulbert sold cheap candy that his family obtained from a salesman known as "the Candy Man."

"I hated selling candy, but it was my mother's way to earn extra money and trade for the bed linens she wanted. Whether I wanted to or not, my mother would load me down with boxes of cheap candy consigned to her by the white 'candy man.' No one really knew the candy man, but like clockwork, at the beginning of the chopping- and picking-cotton sea-

sons, he'd show up. He would have his 1954 Chevrolet piled high with boxes of candy, cheap sheets, red-letter Bibles and cotton print dresses that were never true to their sizes.

No one ever called him by his name. He was just the candy man. Segregation didn't bother him. On a hot dusty day he'd step right into your house, get himself a drink of water and even eat if food was offered."

This type of traveling salesman invariably took advantage of the poor people he served. His merchandise was poorly made and overpriced, but in many cases, he was the only source many poor rural black families had for something "fancy."

fields of dentistry, medicine, and education created special barriers to nonwhites.

Those few lucky and persistent blacks who succeeded in overcoming the obstacles and receiving their professional licenses usually set up their practices in larger cities, and it was there that white professionals met their greatest competition. Prejudice, though, usually limited a black professional's or businessman's clientele to members of the African American community.

Medicine

Prejudice also worked against black physicians in another way; many black patients had a decided preference for white doctors. This preference was due to their assumption that white doctors would have greater access to medical facilities from which black practitioners were excluded. Also, few black physicians would be allowed to consult with their white counterparts on difficult cases. As a result, the few black physicians who practiced in the South did so in the cities and larger towns, where a larger number of black patients might be found.

The difficulties faced by a black physician, especially in the South, were formidable. As one historian relates,

> They arrived at their initial post with few possessions and financial means, many of them still paying off debts accrued from their education. They needed to rent an office or work from their homes and establish a following. They found a mostly impoverished clientele, they needed to compete with established white doctors who might resent their competition, and they sensed with good reason that any mistaken diagnosis or treatment would

immediately call into question their competence to practice medicine. Of the few whites who patronized them, most were poor; in some communities, however, the black physician developed a reputation for treating venereal diseases, attracting whites of all classes. "When a young fellow of the aristocratic class, and this is an aristocratic town, gets syphilis [sic] and gonorrhea," a pharmacist in Tennessee revealed, "he usually goes to this negro [physician] and so avoids the embarrassment of submitting such a case to a friend of the family."[66]

Black professionals faced other barriers as well. A great many hospitals in the South would not permit black doctors and nurses to treat patients there. In addition, local and state chapters of the American Medical Association would not admit black physicians as members.

Law

Black lawyers, even more so than their black colleagues in medicine, had to acknowledge that many black clients preferred to hire a white practitioner who, by virtue of being white, would be able to obtain a greater degree of justice from white judges and juries. Black attorneys were subject to harassment and never knew how they might be treated in court, making the defense of a client that much more difficult. For example, black attorney Samuel A. Beadle, a graduate of Atlanta University and Tougaloo College, reported that in the early years of the twentieth century he received a wide range of treatment in white courtrooms—from acceptance to outright harassment or exclusion. In Yazoo City, Mississippi, he was barred from sitting

A. Philip Randolph

Asa Philip Randolph (1889–1979) played a leading role in the fight for black civil rights from the 1920s through the 1960s. He was also an important American labor leader. In 1925 he founded the Brotherhood of Sleeping Car Porters, a union he headed until 1968. He also served as vice president of the American Federation of Labor and Congress of Industrial Organizations (AFL-CIO). Born in Crescent City, Florida, he moved to New York City as a young man, working odd jobs during the day and attending City College of New York at night.

In 1941 Randolph planned a giant protest march in Washington, D.C., to demand jobs for blacks in defense industries. Partly to appease Randolph and avoid the planned march, President Franklin D. Roosevelt set up the Fair Employment Practices Committee.

In 1963 Randolph's dream of a march on Washington came true when he helped organize the march in which Martin Luther King Jr. made his famous "I Have a Dream" speech. Randolph served as host for the program of speakers that day, and he introduced King to the crowd and to the

In 1941, A. Philip Randolph wanted to organize a giant protest in Washington, D.C. Twenty-two years later that dream came true when he helped organize the March on Washington, which was attended by a quarter of a million people.

world as "the moral leader of our nation." Randolph's funeral in 1979 was attended by labor and political dignitaries from around the world.

---

inside the railing where the court's white officers and attorneys sat. In Columbus, Mississippi, he was not even allowed to enter the courtroom. His life was threatened, and court remained adjourned until he had left the city.

Black Women in the Workplace

African American women faced their own workplace conditions during the Jim Crow era, one of which was the economic necessity of their working in the first place. Unlike white women, most black women had no choice but to work outside the home. By 1870 all but 2 percent of white wives in the rural South defined their occupation as "keeping house." Forty percent of black wives, however, listed their job as "field laborer." Among the poorest sharecropping households during the Jim Crow years, the percentage of black working women approached 90 percent.

Jobs for black women were even more limited than those available for black men. Many black women were excluded from jobs that were considered "man's work." Like their male counterparts, black women who worked outside the home also found that some jobs were considered to be for whites only. Black women were not allowed to be receptionists, secretaries, sales clerks, or waitresses in white-owned businesses. Most southern black women who found jobs did so as field hands or as domestic servants.

A typical black working woman's schedule could be arduous beyond belief:

The notion of the woman's work as never done was grounded in experience. And the experience varied only slightly from household to household. Up at dawn, she cooked breakfast for the family, after which she joined her husband and the grown children in the fields, plowing or chopping cotton. She would return to the cabin in midmorning to cook dinner, clean up, and return to the fields in the early afternoon and work until sundown. In the evening, she might also be expected to milk the cows and feed the chickens before preparing supper, after

Black women were not even allowed such jobs as receptionists, sales clerks, or waitresses, but found work as domestic servants or field hands.

which she performed household chores, such as mending, making, washing, and ironing clothes, and scrubbing floors.[67]

White families depended on the availability of low-paid black women to help in their homes. Many times black men were denied jobs simply to keep them dependent on their wives working as domestic maids and servants in white households. One farmworker recalled the situation in Anthony Walton's *Mississippi: An American Journey:*

> They [whites] wanted us just scraping by. They knew if we had factory jobs, when we got home we was gonna want our suppers done, too. We was gonna want our cold water. We gon' want our houses clean. We was gonna have a little extra here, a little extra there, and our wives wasn't gonna have time to spend eight hours out yonder taking care of their babies. She'd take care of her own babies.[68]

Success for a Black Person

Despite Jim Crow restrictions, some blacks actually succeeded in business; some even prospered. But wealth did not necessarily lead to security for black families. In the South, a prosperous black man became the target of whites who were jealous of his success. In 1903 a former governor of North Carolina observed that

> the Negro who gets very prosperous is to be pitied, for straightaway he is in a situation where danger confronts him. Let him own a fine farm, blooded horses and cattle, and dare to ride in a carriage, and if I were an insurance agent I would not make out a policy on his life.[69]

The Ku Klux Klan often singled out successful blacks who they suspected of having saved their earnings. "If you got so you made good money an' had a good farm," Pierce Harper, a former slave from North Carolina, recalled, "de Klu Klux'd come an' murder you." He had seen it happen to his neighbor, Jim Freeman: "Dey taken him an' destroyed his stuff an' him 'cause he was making some money. Hung him on a tree in his front yard, right in front of his cabin."[70] Many blacks at the beginning of the twentieth century saw little hope for success and security in the South, even if they had the good fortune to be financially successful. For that reason, and for many others, they moved north.

Black Migration from the South

During the first three decades of the twentieth century, younger blacks, many of whom had served in the military in World War I and had received at least a measure of respect from the Europeans they had met, began to search for an alternative to the degradation of the Jim Crow South. Many black workers migrated to the North, seeking better jobs and hoping for a better life for their families.

At the same time, other factors conspired to eliminate black jobs in the South. Labor shortages in southern cotton fields during World War I helped spur the development of mechanized farm equipment. When chemical weed killers and cotton-picking machines became commonplace in the South, the number of unskilled farm jobs dropped dramatically. As a result of these technological developments, and because of their recent exposure to the more tolerant racial attitudes they found outside the South, thousands of blacks left southern states during and after the war

The White Citizens Council

In 1954 the U.S. Supreme Court ordered all public schools to be integrated. To preserve their superior position in society, many white southerners increased the pressure on blacks, both political and economic, to force them to stay "in their place." Whites launched a two-pronged attack against desegregation using random violence and the revival of the Ku Klux Klan to instill fear in the black community. A new group, the White Citizens Council, made up of prominent politicians, professionals, and business leaders, placed economic pressure on blacks and whites alike to toe the racial line. This "white-collar Klan" made it impossible for anyone who favored desegregation to find or keep a job in the South, buy anything on credit, secure a bank loan, or get a mortgage.

years. Most headed north to Chicago and other Midwestern cities, drawn by the hope of a factory job.

However, the great migration of blacks into the residential slum areas and the industrial plants of big northern cities led to an increase of tension between the races in the North. White northern laborers were protective of their status and resented competition from blacks. Blacks were pushed out of the more desirable industrial jobs they had been able to acquire during World War I. Some found a better life, but many had to put their hopes aside as they labored once again in the menial jobs no one else wanted. Whether in the North or in the South, blacks were at the mercy of a white-dominated society; without an official voice in how that society functioned—in other words, without the vote—their hopes would remain unfulfilled.

"And Justice for All"

Racial discrimination and segregation were the rule for black people when they dealt with government agencies in the age of Jim Crow, just as they were in education and in the workplace. For blacks, running for public office, voting, sitting on a jury, or being arrested and tried for a crime were totally different experiences than they were for whites.

Voting Restrictions

When states were required by the Fourteenth and subsequently the Fifteenth Amendments to give blacks the right to vote, they discovered that the law said nothing about what requirements citizens had to meet to be able to exercise their right to vote. Federal law did not prevent states from imposing poll taxes and complicated literacy tests with questions requiring potential voters to explain various portions of the state constitution before being allowed to vote. When blacks actually passed these tests (a rare occurrence), they were sometimes required to place their ballots in boxes separate from the ballots of whites. It was not until 1965 that the use of such tests and devices was outlawed by the federal Voting Rights Act.

The most common devices used by southern states to prevent blacks from voting were originally used in Mississippi during Reconstruction and were part of the Mississippi Plan. The plan set up barriers for black voters, such as property or literacy requirements, then created certain loopholes through which only white voters could squeeze. The loopholes allowing underprivileged whites to vote were the "understanding clause," the "grandfather clause," or the "good character clause." Grandfather clauses gave the right to vote to anyone who had been able to vote on January 1, 1867, along with their direct descendants. Since the vast majority of blacks had not yet voted by that year, they were excluded from the voting booth.

In addition, all southern states—members of the old Confederacy—adopted poll taxes, to be paid by voters when they registered. This was the most reliable means of preventing anyone from voting who represented a threat to white landowners—blacks and poor whites. In most states the poll taxes amounted to about five dollars, but to someone who was paid from forty cents to two dollars per day, depending on the year, this was enough to deter voting by many blacks.

The U.S. Constitution guaranteed the right to vote, but southern states used these means to prevent blacks from *registering* to vote. Although technically legal, the practice of limiting voter registration was still discriminatory. And if a black person did learn to read, acquired sufficient property, was able to pay the poll tax, and kept the tax receipt on file, a final hurdle remained: the white primary election.

By law a political party's candidates for office were selected in a primary election open

Blacks are taught how to fill out registration forms to increase black voting power, which has been low since the Jim Crow era and literacy tests.

only to party members. The Democratic Party was overwhelmingly dominant in the South, and federal law did not require the Democratic primary election to include black voters. As far as the federal government was concerned, political parties were private organizations and could exclude from membership whomever they pleased. As a result, any black person who succeeded in registering to vote in the South was faced, on election day, with a ballot containing only white candidates' names. The unavoidable fact was that his or her vote would not make any difference in the outcome of the election.

One example of the effectiveness of Jim Crow laws in depriving black citizens the right to vote is the number of registered black voters in Louisiana in 1896—130,334—compared with those in 1904—1,342. Between these two dates, the literacy, property, and poll-tax qualifications were adopted. In Louisiana in 1896, black registered voters were in the majority in twenty-six parishes. By 1900, even though the black population of the state had increased, they were not the majority in any parish.

Literacy Tests and the Power of the Registrar

Blacks often found that being able to read did them little good when they arrived at the polls. Officials in charge of voter registration, the registrars, often asked questions that made no sense or were irrelevant, such as "How old was Christ when he was born?" or "How many windows are there in the White House?" The anecdotal history of blacks' almost impossible struggle to register to vote in the South is best illustrated by a story quoted by Lawrence Levine in *Black Culture and Black Consciousness: Afro American Folk Thought from Slavery to Freedom* and further documented by historian Leon F. Litwack. The story tells of a black man who tried to register to vote somewhere in Mississippi. When he actually passed the literacy test, the registrars momentarily became flustered. After a quick conference among themselves, they showed him a headline printed in Chinese and asked him if he knew what it meant.

"Yeah, I know what it means," he replied. "It means that niggers don't vote in Mississippi again this year."[71]

Voter registrars had enormous power to decide whether someone could be considered literate. Roger T. Stevenson, who was a voting official in Seaboard, North Carolina, for a quarter of a century, recalled using his power as a registrar to judge the qualifications of voters. According to Stevenson, he could always find a way to fail someone on a literacy test:

Some wrote [copied from memory] the Constitution, I reckon, as good as a lot o' white men, but I'd find somethin' unsatisfactory, maybe an *i* not dotted or a *t* not crossed, enough for me to disqualify 'em. The law said "satisfactory to the registrar."[72]

Purging the Rolls

Should blacks succeed in getting their names on the list of qualified voters, their troubles had usually just begun. For one thing, their names could be purged, or removed, from the list before they got a chance to vote. In Georgia, for example, the purge procedure was quite simple. Black people would be sent a legal summons to appear before the county board of registrars at a specified time—almost always during working hours—to "show cause" why their names should not be dropped because of "bad character, criminal record,"[73] or other reasons. If they failed to appear, their names were automatically stricken from the rolls. Even if they did appear at the hearing, their names sometimes mysteriously disappeared from the rolls anyway, at the whim of the registrar. In Florida, black voters were supposed to be sent a postcard that they had to sign and return in order

Cracking, Stacking, and Packing the Black Vote

Black political progress after Reconstruction was slowed by whites in several ways. Taken together, the practices were known as cracking, stacking, and packing. One method involved the redrawing of voting district lines in such a way that blacks would not be in the majority in any district. Such a practice of cracking or diluting black voting power is also called gerrymandering.

Stacking was another form of gerrymandering in which a large number of blacks would be included in a district with even more white voters. Packing involved, in the rare instances in which blacks could not otherwise be silenced, drawing the district so it was totally black, thus ensuring that neighboring areas would provide safe white seats that would outvote the black representative.

for their names not to be stricken. Failure to receive such a card on time was not an acceptable excuse. Usually, due to late mailing by the registrar's office, or the cooperation of local white postal employees, blacks did not receive the cards in time.

A Campaign of Terror

When laws and loopholes failed to keep blacks from voting, other tactics, including the threat of losing one's job and the terror of lynching, proved just as effective even as recently as the 1950s. Since almost all employers were white, the economic threat was quite real. For example, a teaching position in an all-black school was one of the only good jobs a black person could obtain. A white board of education and a white superintendent always controlled teaching jobs in those schools, though, and any hint that a black teacher was trying to register to vote would almost surely lead to his or her dismissal. Even a person hired to pick cotton on a white-owned farm or clean and cook in a white household could easily find that voting, or just registering to vote, could lead to the loss of the black family's only source of income.

Fannie Lou Hamer, the civil rights activist from Mississippi, recalls how rural blacks in Mississippi felt about the risks they faced when they tried to vote, and why many felt voting was not worth the risk:

> Few could worry about voting when there were almost no jobs left picking cotton and no proper schooling to qualify a black person for whatever jobs did exist. Few could worry about voting when children went hungry and rain poured through holes in the roof, or when children died in fires caused by primitive stoves in unheated shacks. Or when people went to the hospital only to die. Or when the white world was deliberately leaving blacks further behind, and when its rear guard of white sheriffs turned their dogs on those trying to assert their rights, and men riding at night fired shotguns at them or tried to burn down their barns.[74]

The threat of being lynched by a mob of angry whites was an understandably effective deterrent to blacks who might otherwise desire to cast their ballots. Lynchings became so commonplace in the South during the first three decades of the twentieth century that they were sometimes advertised in newspapers, providing a grisly spectator sport. Needless to say, if black citizens were not willing to risk losing their job to vote, they certainly would not risk being lynched in order to vote.

"Call to Arms"

Each state in the South had its own way of dealing with what local officials called the "problem" of black voting during the Jim Crow era. Some used force; others relied on intimidation. Whatever their method, the results were the same—few blacks voted.

Around the turn of the century, typical of the techniques employed to keep blacks from voting was the following "Call to Arms" issued on election eve in North Carolina:

> You are Anglo-Saxons. You are armed and prepared and you will do your duty. Go to the polls tomorrow and if you find the Negro voting tell him to leave the polls and if he refuses, kill him, shoot him down in his tracks. We shall win tomorrow if we have to do it with guns.[75]

When Georgia's liberal governor Ellis Arnall abolished the state's poll tax in 1947, an opposing candidate for the office, Eugene Talmadge, declared: "I done decided the best way to keep the niggers from voting is to let all the white folks vote, and then pass the word around that Mister Nigger is not wanted at the polls."[76] Likewise, Mississippi senator Theodore Bilbo, in a statewide election-eve broadcast from Jackson on June 23, 1945, urged "every red-blooded Mississippian to use every means at their command"[77] to keep blacks from the polls.

Individuals in some states became rather creative in their approach to the "black voting problem." In Miami, Florida, for example, Klansmen strung up effigies bearing placards that read, "This Nigger Voted." They

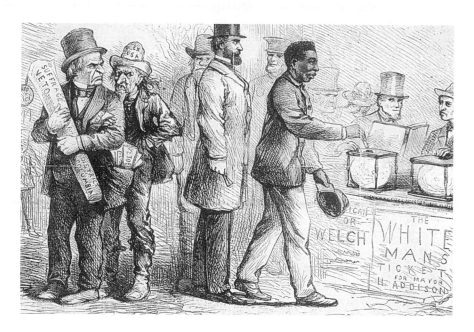

When the few blacks who did vote went to the polls, they were threatened, beaten, and sometimes killed.

also distributed calling cards reading, "Respectable Negro Citizens Not Voting Tomorrow; Niggers Stay Away from the Polls!" In Fitzgerald, Georgia, the KKK tacked notices to black church doors reading, "The First Nigger who Votes will be a Dead Nigger."[78]

When the few brave registered black voters arrived at southern voting polls, they sometimes found whites nearby, threatening them with firearms. Physical attacks on black voters were not uncommon. Blacks were attacked when they emerged from the polling booth, or somewhat later, as was the case with Isaiah Nixon of Montgomery County, Georgia, in the mid-1940s. He voted, even though white election officials warned him against it, and later that night was shot to death in his home in front of his wife and children.

Black Justice?

In the courts as well as at the polls, southern justice was applied unequally. When whites victimized blacks, they often escaped trial, even

for serious offenses. Nearly any white person could avoid being tried for a crime, even murder, if the victim was black. In murder cases, the courts ruled that the killing of a black by a white was justifiable. Even if brought to trial and convicted, sentences handed to white convicts reflected white southerners' notions of the value of a black's life.

For a black defendant, on the other hand, even minor infractions of the law could lead to long jail sentences. Once in trouble with the law, a black person knew not to expect equal treatment. In the local jail, the court, and the state prison, he or she faced the harshest forms of discrimination.

During the Jim Crow years, many blacks—young and old, men, women, and children—were held in city jails for no reason other than to be "taught a lesson," and southern jailers usually employed pain to get their message across. According to Chalmers Archer Jr., who grew up in rural Mississippi,

It was a time when police would brutally bend wrists and fingers of black people.

Fannie Lou Hamer and Voter Registration in Mississippi

Fannie Lou Hamer was born into a family of impoverished Mississippi sharecroppers. She was almost forty-five years old when she first tried to register to vote. When Hamer arrived at the courthouse, Circuit Clerk Cecil Campbell was hostile when she told him that she and a group of African Americans had come to register. He said that all but two of the group would have to leave, so Hamer and Ernest Davis stayed to take the literacy test.

A prospective voter had to fill out a long questionnaire with personal information, and it had to be written just right, with every *t* crossed and every *i* dotted. She also had to put down on the form where she worked, and she knew why. "Well, see, when you put by whom you are employed, you fired by the time you get back home." Finally, the registrar would bring out a big black book and ask the potential voter to interpret a section of the state constitution. Registrars could use this method to pass those they wanted to pass and fail any others. According to Hamer, whites passed but blacks rarely did.

In Hamer's case, the clerk pointed to the sixteenth section of the Mississippi Constitution, a section dealing with obscure laws. Hamer said it dealt with "facto" laws, and that she "knowed about as much about a facto law as a horse knows about Christmas Day." She flunked the test.

When Hamer died on March 14, 1977, she was still poor and still made her home in the Mississippi Delta. Her funeral, though, was attended by hundreds of dignitaries from around the world. Andrew Young, the civil rights leader and former U.S. ambassador to the United Nations, delivered Hamer's eulogy, praising her strength and courage.

Fannie Lou Hamer was forty-five years old when she first tried to register to vote, but was denied when she failed the literacy test.

Stories from jail were a litany of pain and unusual punishments. I personally still feel the splitting pain inflicted by the police only because I did not get off the sidewalk while passing a white woman.[79]

Archer also wrote that when white officers would handcuff blacks, they would tighten the cuffs so much that the black prisoner's wrists would become swollen or even broken.

Dealing with "the Man"

During the decades of Jim Crow, statistics show that poor blacks were subjected to more frequent arrests and more severe treatment at the hands of "the Man"—the police—than whites or upper- or middle-class blacks. In most of the South, blacks had to conform to a completely different set of rules than whites.

Both Atlanta, Georgia, and Clarksdale, Mississippi, maintained curfews during the 1930s and 1940s that were rigidly enforced, but only for blacks. Even in cities without curfews, accosting blacks on the street and subjecting them to ridicule and abuse became a favorite sport for white police officers.

The threat of going to jail was often enough to force a black person to comply with even the vaguest order from a local police officer. According to Martin Luther King Jr., in *Why We Can't Wait,*

Jailing the Negro was once as much a threat as the loss of a job. To any Negro who displayed a spark of manhood, a southern law-enforcement officer could say: "Nigger, watch your step, or I'll put you in jail." The Negro knew what going to jail meant. It meant not only confinement and isolation from his loved ones. It meant that at the jailhouse he could probably expect a severe beating. And it meant that his day in court, if he had it, would be a mockery of justice.[80]

Blacks were often subjected to arrest and suffered severe treatment by police if they did not conform to the rules set for them.

A black person in the southern United States found more equality on paper during the Jim Crow era than in reality. The Fourteenth and Fifteenth Amendments to the U.S. Constitution guaranteed blacks equality, but in the South, local statutes managed to nullify many of those rights. The basis of second-class citizenship for southern blacks was not just in the local laws, it was also in the way those laws were administered. An African American might technically be the equal of any white under the Constitution, but not on southern streets and not before the bar of southern justice.

An innocent black man could be caught in a police dragnet and tortured into confessing a crime he never committed. And his troubles would just be starting if he were sent to prison. Stories abound of the brutality and unfairness of southern white policemen and their treatment of black prisoners. During the waning years of the Jim Crow era, for example, thousands of activists in the civil rights movement, both black and white, were taken to jail, sometimes without being charged with a crime. Once there, they were subjected to beatings, held for long periods of time in dark cells without being allowed to call a lawyer, and sometimes killed.

Being beaten and humiliated in jail was preferable to what might happen if a white mob took the law into their own hands, however. Lynching was the ultimate form of social control, and neither youth nor old age nor social class offered protection to blacks who did not stay "in their place."

The Reign of "Colonel Lynch"

Victims of lynch mobs had usually challenged, or in one way or another violated, some aspect of white supremacy. These violations, whether intentional or unintentional, ranged from trivial to serious (at least in the eyes of whites). Several examples are recounted in Leon F. Litwack's *Trouble in Mind:*

> Charles Jones, a youth from Grovetown, Georgia, was lynched by 150 whites for stealing a pair of shoes and "talking big." Henry Sykes was lynched in Okolona, Mississippi, for calling up white girls on the telephone and annoying them. A Texas youth was jailed for writing an insulting letter to a young white woman; a mob broke into the jail and shot him to death. Jeff Brown accidentally brushed against a white girl as he was running to catch a train; a mob hanged him for "attempted rape." For their "utter worthlessness," John Shaw and George Call, two eighteen-year-old youths from Lynchburg, Virginia, were shot to death after the mob's attempt to hang them failed.[81]

These illegal executions, often carried out with the full knowledge and cooperation of local police, were intended to punish real or imagined offenses by blacks: standing up for themselves, having a disagreement with a white man in a business dealing, theft (sometimes petty theft), murder, and, most often, raping or being too friendly toward a white woman or merely making one of them feel uncomfortable.

Many times, political leaders—judges, sheriffs, jailers, and local police—stood by helplessly during a lynching or, at times, actively participated. It was fairly common for members of a lynch mob to pose for a photograph with the sheriff and the intended victim before the lynching or with the body of the victim afterward.

The incidence of lynching reached its peak in the 1880s and 1890s. There were 230

Lynchings were illegal executions, but they were often carried out with the full knowledge of the local police and sheriff.

lynchings reported in 1892, the highest number recorded for the nation. Since this figure reflects only those lynchings reported to the federal government and to city newspapers, the actual figure may be higher. Mississippi recorded the highest total of any state, 581 lynchings from 1882 to 1996, with 539 of the victims being black.

Nothing emphasized more dramatically the low value placed on black life in the South than the practice of lynching. As one black Mississippian recalls,

Back in those days [the 1930s, but it could apply equally as well to the late nineteenth century and most of the first half of the twentieth century], to kill a Negro wasn't nothing. It was like killing a chicken or killing a snake. The whites would say, "Niggers jest supposed to die, ain't no damn good anyway—so jest go on an' kill 'em."

Another black southerner adds, "In those days it was 'Kill a mule, buy another. Kill a nigger, hire another.' They had to have a license to kill anything but a nigger. We was always in season."[82]

A Day in Court

Even if a black accused of a crime managed to escape the lynch mob and make it into court, he or she could not expect many sympathetic faces. Nowhere in the South did blacks take part in administering judicial institutions. There were no black judges, few black officers of the law, and no blacks serving in clerical positions in official agencies. C. Vann Woodward, in a 1974 study of the Jim Crow years, notes that

> the Negro's rights were curtailed in the courts as well as at the polls. By custom or by law Negroes were excluded from jury service. . . . The ban against Negro jurors, witnesses, and judges, as well as the economic degradation of the race, help to explain the disproportionate numbers of Negroes in . . . prisons and the heavy limitations on the protection of Negro life, liberty, and property.[83]

Southern courts, along with the police, enforced the Jim Crow system. Once social customs became law in the South, it was essential that any person guilty of a violation be quickly punished to serve as an example to others of how the system should be maintained. In addition, any black person who claimed to have been wronged by a white person and tried to find justice within the system soon found that the system favored whites.

One example of this lesson in southern justice occurred in 1897. A black woman in Hinds County, Mississippi, charged a white man with beating her with an ax handle. The justice of the peace who heard the case told her that he could not find a law stating it was illegal for a white man to beat a black woman, so he set the white man free.

In the South, it seemed that justice came in two colors, and it varied according to the race of the victim as well as the race of the criminal. According to Litwack,

> If a black person killed a white man, according to "Negro law," he would suffer death "in some form or other, the time, place and manner of his execution depending altogether on who caught him, the sheriff's posse or the friends of the deceased." But if a black person killed a black person, the "usual practice" was to appoint "some young inexperienced attorney" to take his case, allow the defendant to plead guilty, and sentence him to life imprisonment. The community thereby saved the expense of a drawn-out trial, the defendant escaped hanging, and the state secured still another convict whose labor could be sold to augment the annual revenue.[84]

Strict segregation was maintained in the courtrooms. In the Johnston County, North Carolina, courthouse, for example, blacks, both as observers and as participants, could sit only in the balcony while whites sat downstairs. Black witnesses were allowed to come downstairs only when called. No detail of the legal proceeding was too trivial to escape segregation's effects. There was even one Bible for white witnesses to swear on and another for black witnesses to use.

Black defendants in the Jim Crow criminal justice system confronted hurdles that few could overcome. When they entered the courtroom, they faced a white judge and jury eager to convict, sometimes on the flimsiest of evidence. Many times, white judges and juries were unwilling to believe the testimony of black defendants or black witnesses. Ned Cobb, who was born in Alabama in 1885, sums up the black experience in a southern court of law:

[A] nigger could go in court and testify against his own color in favor of the white man, and his word was took. But when it come to speakin out in his own defense, nigger weren't heard in court. White folks is white folks, niggers is niggers, and a nigger's word never has went worth a penny unless some white man backed it up and told the same thing that the nigger told and was willin to stand up for the nigger. But if another white man spoke against the nigger and against the white man that was supportin him, why, they'd call that first white man "nigger-lover" and they wouldn't believe a word he said.[85]

Even if there were doubts on the minds of the judge and jury about the defendant's guilt, many rushed to judgment to avoid the peril of mob violence. One extreme case involved Lawson Davis, a black Mississippian who allegedly attempted to enter the bedroom of a white woman. Despite an almost total lack of evidence, he was barely saved from being lynched. Fearing for his life, he was persuaded to plead guilty to sexual assault. In just seven minutes, an all-white jury was impaneled, evidence was presented, and a sentence of ninety-nine years in prison was imposed.

In addition to the fear of private vengeance, many white judges and juries were sometimes intimidated by the overwhelming presence of Ku Klux Klan members in the courtroom. Not many southern whites were

willing to risk the wrath of the Klan for delaying "swift justice" on blacks accused of crimes against whites.

Blacks faced an all-too-familiar double standard in courts of law. The courts prosecuted some black crimes inconsistently, depending on the situation. Punishment for theft, for example, depended on what was stolen, from whom it was stolen, and whether or not the black person's employer wanted him or her on the job. Blacks accused of vagrancy and drunkenness faced the same inconsistency. Sometimes they were prosecuted harshly, and sometimes they were released by judges who considered such behavior merely a racial defect.

Some crimes committed by one race might not be punishable when committed by the other. Judges and juries often ignored offenses committed by whites against blacks or showed leniency in sentencing. A black person could almost always expect to serve far more jail time and pay a much heavier fine than a white person arrested for the same offense. According to one historian,

For conviction on a petty theft charge, a black might have to stay several years in the penitentiary, often because he was unable to pay the fine and court costs; a white man would most likely serve no more than ninety days in the county jail or pay a small fine and be reprimanded.[86]

Forced Labor in Southern Prisons

With southern justice so weighted against blacks, and with jail sentences for black defendants so severe, jails and prisons remained full—mostly with black prisoners. Traditionally even petty crimes were punished by long sentences of hard labor. Some prisoners were forced to work on chain gangs while others were leased out as convict labor to work for private companies. They worked in coal and iron mines, in sawmills, and in forests tapping pine trees for turpentine. They laid railroad tracks, built levees, grew cotton, and cleared swampland.

The majority of prisoners in the South who were sentenced to spend time on these gangs were black men. Across the South, states and local plantation owners benefitted from this updated form of slavery.

What Black People Learned from the White Man's Law

During the Jim Crow years, young blacks learned at an early age that in the South "white justice" and "black justice" were hardly equal. They learned from their own experiences, and from those of their parents and grandparents before them, that the police and the courts existed to enforce blacks' second-class status instead of to protect them and their rights as citizens. They learned to have little faith in the white man's law or sense of fair play. While white children usually considered a policeman a friend and protector, black children learned to fear him as an enemy.

According to W. E. B. Du Bois in 1903,

Daily the Negro is coming more and more to look upon law and justice, not as protecting safeguards, but as sources of humiliation and oppression. The laws are made by men who have little interest in him; they are executed by men who have absolutely no motive for treating the black people with courtesy or consideration; and, finally, the accused law-breaker

Southern Vagrancy Laws

Although the U.S. Constitution did not guarantee a person's right to work, every state had so-called vagrancy laws that made it a criminal offense to be without work. On the surface, these laws said nothing about race, but since they were administered during the Jim Crow era, they had everything to do with race. Seldom enforced against whites, vagrancy laws provided a steady supply of black labor for highway maintenance and for the harvest of southern crops.

The crime of vagrancy, as it was administered in the South, was regarded as an ongoing one, which meant a person could be sent to jail over and over on the same charge as long as he or she remained broke and unemployed. In most states the penalty for persons convicted of vagrancy was a fine ranging from fifty dollars to one hundred dollars, and/or a thirty-day jail sentence, usually on a public chain gang. Each state allowed its prisoners to "work off" their jail time, but the rates varied. Arkansas state law, for example, specified that vagrancy fines would be worked off at the archaic rate of one dollar per day.

In fact, southern police forces often arrested weekly quotas of blacks, despite whether they had actually committed crimes, to fill out their local chain gangs. Throughout the South, vagrancy laws took the place of the Black Codes that were instituted by white planters shortly after the Civil War and were aimed at keeping blacks in a state of semislavery.

is tried, not by his peers, but too often by men who would rather punish ten innocent Negroes than let one guilty one escape.[87]

As unfair as the South's electoral process and judicial system were toward blacks, it was within the court system itself that Jim Crow laws were fought and eventually brought down. First through the courts, then through the ballot box, blacks and concerned whites made gains throughout the 1950s and 1960s, bringing the Jim Crow system to an end and achieving justice and equality for everyone.

The Civil Rights Movement and the End of Jim Crow

The years 1954 through 1968 are known in the United States as the years of the civil rights movement. After more than half a century of life under Jim Crow, blacks and a few whites took a stand for equality and demanded equal treatment as guaranteed in the U.S. Constitution. These were tense years, filled with violent resistance to change, hatred, sorrow, and persecution for many civil rights activists, both black and white. Blacks persisted in their demands until the Jim Crow laws were abolished, and a new era was born—that of legally mandated equality in social treatment and economic opportunity, in education and in the workplace.

Origins in Wartime

By the end of World War II, the attitudes of America's white fighting men toward black soldiers showed signs of changing. After observing black soldiers in combat, a large percentage of the officers and enlisted men came to believe that, with identical training, black soldiers would be just as effective as white

Although there were all-black infantries in World War I (pictured), it was not until white and black soldiers fought along side each other in World War II and Korea that the attitude of whites toward blacks started to change.

ones. It took a presidential order to end segregation in the nation's armed forces, however.

Mixing the Races

On July 26, 1948, President Harry S. Truman signed Executive Order 9981 calling for "equality of treatment and opportunity for all persons in the armed forces without regard to race, color, or national origin."[88] As a new war raged in Korea, true integration in the armed forces took place. In 1950 General Matthew Ridgeway, commander of the American forces in Korea, requested permission to integrate all troops under his command. After this was accomplished, race relations, contrary to the fears of many, took a turn for the better, as did the effectiveness of the integrated troops. Soldiers discovered that the race of their comrades really did not matter. As one young white officer remarked,

I was in the Pacific two years, and I can tell you, I don't know about there not being any atheists in foxholes, but I know damned well there weren't any segregationists in the ones I saw. When you're looking forward to being blown to bits any minute, you're so glad to have anybody stick beside you I guess it makes you plumb color blind. I figure if we can get along together when we're in trouble, we ought to be able to do as well here.[89]

Tested under fire during wartime, the new policy was rapidly applied to troops stationed at American military bases throughout the world. The new policy was also encouraged at home. It was applied on army training camps in the Carolinas and Georgia, at air bases in Alabama and Texas, and at naval bases in Virginia and Florida. Black officers were put in the position of giving orders to whites as well as white officers giving orders

Race relations took a turn for the better during the Korean War, when General Matthew Ridgeway requested permission to integrate all troops under his command.

to black soldiers. The policy was extended to civilian employees as well as military personnel, to the base housing of officers' families as well as to the schools for their children. Integration in the military extended beyond combat units and military offices; it included sleeping and eating arrangements, bars, officers' clubs, athletic fields, and swimming pools.

Coming Home

The long-range significance of the military policy of full integration extended far beyond the armed services. As hundreds of thousands of men were discharged from the services and reentered civilian life, they brought with them interracial experiences very few American citizens, northern or southern, ever would have had elsewhere. Soldiers came home with changed attitudes. Black veterans were no longer willing to knuckle under to the humiliation and discrimination of segregation, and white veterans were less inclined to view themselves as superior only because of their skin color. But the Jim Crow system was still firmly entrenched; it would take more direct action by the federal government to end almost a century's tradition.

The Supreme Court and Jim Crow Schools

On May 17, 1954, partly due to the change in attitudes brought back by blacks and whites returning from military service, and partly due to convincing psychological and sociological studies on the effects of segregation, the U.S. Supreme Court decided that its fifty-eight-year-old decision *Plessy v. Ferguson* needed to be overturned. Chief Justice Earl

In Brown v. Board of Education, *Chief Justice Earl Warren delivered the Supreme Court's unanimous decision to overturn* Plessy v. Ferguson, *which had allowed segregation.*

Warren delivered the Court's unanimous opinion in favor of black plaintiffs in the landmark school desegregation case *Brown v. Board of Education:*

> Segregation of white and colored children in public schools has a detrimental effect upon the colored children, [for it] generates a feeling of inferiority as to their status in the community that may affect their hearts and minds in a way unlikely ever to be undone. . . . We conclude that in the field of public education the doctrine of "separate but equal" has no place. Separate facilities are inherently unequal.[90]

Richard Wright, America's Native Son

Richard Wright, who was born in Natchez, Mississippi, in 1908, knew about growing up black in a Jim Crow society. He wrote about the black experience in America in his dramatic 1940 novel *Native Son* and in his autobiography *Black Boy*. *Native Son* tells the story of Bigger Thomas, a young black man whose family had migrated from the South and who now lived with them in the slums of Chicago, attempting to survive under the burden of segregation and discrimination.

"The problem of living as a Negro was cold and hard. What was it that made the hate of whites for blacks so steady, seemingly so woven into the texture of things? What kind of life was possible under that hate? How had this hate come to be? Nothing about the problems of Negroes was ever taught in the classrooms at school."

The raw power of Richard Wright's books and their effects on his readers are best illustrated by the comments of a young white superintendent of schools from a rural county in the South, which were quoted in the 1957 study *Neither Black nor White.*

"My own attitude toward the whole race question has changed completely, and I know just when it happened. I'd been born and grown up here, never known or thought anything different from what everyone else did; it was the same way when I went to the state university.

Then during [World War II], I joined the Navy. At first I stayed away from the two or three Negroes we had on shipboard. I argued with a lot of the northern boys about race—they always bring it up when a southerner's around. I just didn't get near the Negroes if I could help it. I don't know what I'd have done if one had been assigned to bunk with me right there at the first.

Well, . . . one day [a] Massachusetts boy gave me a book to read. It was Richard Wright's *Black Boy*. Reading that book opened my eyes. I'd never thought before about what a Negro feels like growing up in the South. I looked at those Negroes on shipboard closer after that; even got to know them pretty well. And through the years since I've come to look at Negroes as people, one, two, three. That's all it takes."

The Supreme Court's decision was the most momentous and far-reaching civil rights decision of the century. It marked the beginning of the end of Jim Crow. But the end was to be agonizingly slow in coming.

The Movement

The sweeping effort to end Jim Crow, known as the civil rights movement, began in 1955 when a black seamstress named Rosa Parks refused to give up her seat on a bus to a white passenger in Birmingham, Alabama. She was arrested for her defiance of the law. A group of black leaders took this event as their chance to call attention to the racism blacks had suffered under throughout the United States.

Leaders of this movement included Martin Luther King Jr., Asa Philip Randolph, Ralph Abernathy, Jesse Jackson, Andrew Young, Rosa Parks, Fannie Lou Hamer, Medgar Evers, and dozens of other men and women who were determined to see African Americans receive equal treatment after suffering decades of abuse.

After almost a century of living under Jim Crow, African Americans decided they had had enough. They chose nonviolent disobedience as their tool for protest. In his "Letter from a Birmingham Jail," King writes:

You may well ask: "Why direct action? Why sit-ins, marches and so forth? Isn't negotiation a better path?". . . Nonviolent direct action seeks to create such a crisis and foster such a tension that a community which has constantly refused to negotiate is forced to confront the issue. It seeks so to dramatize the issue that it can no longer be ignored.[91]

Free at Last

After years of struggle, the strategy worked. New federal legislation, a sympathetic Supreme Court, and an increase in public awareness and support for the civil rights cause brought an end to Jim Crow laws in the South as well as a gradual end to de facto segregation in the North. Never again would black people allow themselves to be summarily oppressed because of the color of their skin. And because of their example, never again would members of any minority allow themselves to be oppressed because of their religion, their ethnic heritage, their gender, or their sexual preference.

The end of the Jim Crow laws did not bring about instant happiness and prosperity

By refusing to give up her seat on a bus to a white passenger, Rosa Parks triggered the civil rights movement, which brought an end to much segregation.

Thurgood Marshall and *Brown v. Board of Education*

Thurgood Marshall led a team of NAACP lawyers before the U.S. Supreme Court in 1954, arguing a group of court cases collectively known as *Brown v. Board of Education*. These cases involved various black students from across the country who wanted to attend white schools but were prevented from doing so because of segregation laws. In the landmark case, Marshall succeeded in convincing the all-white justices that school segregation should be abolished.

Born in Baltimore, Maryland, in 1908, Marshall graduated from Lincoln University and studied law at Howard University. Appointed to the Supreme Court by President Lyndon B. Johnson in 1967, Marshall became the nation's first black Supreme Court justice. Marshall died on January 24, 1993.

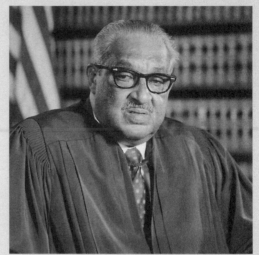

In Brown v. Board of Education, *Thurgood Marshall was able to convince the U.S. Supreme Court that school segregation should be abolished.*

for all blacks. Decades of diminished opportunity, especially in education and job training, had left many African Americans with job skills inferior to those of whites, making it difficult for them to compete for jobs.

Enormous strides have been made in the past three decades. Some plans have worked while others have failed, but progress has been steady. At last, blacks are being recognized for their vital roles in history, the arts, and the sciences. Since the civil rights movement of the 1950s and 1960s, sweeping changes have oc-curred in the South as well as in the rest of the country. However, many of the same prejudices still exist and much work remains to be done.

In the words of Martin Luther King Jr.,

Like life, racial understanding is not something that we find but something that we must create. And so the ability of Negroes and whites to work together, to understand each other, will not be found readymade; it must be created by the fact of contact.[92]

Notes

Introduction: Jim Crow: An American Disgrace

1. Quoted in Anthony Walton, *Mississippi: An American Journey.* New York: Vintage Books, 1996, p. 240.
2. Quoted in Walton, *Mississippi,* p. 240.
3. Quoted in Kenneth C. Davis, *Don't Know Much About History: Everything You Need to Know About American History but Never Learned.* New York: Avon Books, 1990, p. 214.
4. Quoted in Davis, *Don't Know Much About History,* p. 214.
5. Quoted in Leon F. Litwack, *Trouble in Mind: Black Southerners in the Age of Jim Crow.* New York: Alfred A. Knopf, 1998, pp. xiii–xiv.

Chapter 1: The History of Jim Crow

6. C. Vann Woodward, *The Strange Career of Jim Crow,* 3rd ed. New York: Oxford University Press, 1974, p. 12.
7. W. E. B. Du Bois, *The Souls of Black Folk.* 1903. Reprint, New York: Bantam, 1989, p. 128.
8. Chalmers Archer Jr., *Growing Up Black in Rural Mississippi: Memories of a Family, Heritage of a Place.* New York: Walker, 1992, pp. 84–85.
9. Kenneth M. Stampp, *The Era of Reconstruction: 1865–1877.* New York: Vintage Books, 1965, p. 14.
10. Stampp, *The Era of Reconstruction,* p. 80.
11. Quoted in Stampp, *The Era of Reconstruction,* p. 80.
12. Quoted in Stampp, *The Era of Reconstruction,* p. 88.
13. Archer, *Growing Up Black in Rural Mississippi,* p. 82.
14. Archer, *Growing Up Black in Rural Mississippi,* p. 82.
15. Quoted in Woodward, *The Strange Career of Jim Crow,* p. 33.
16. Stampp, *The Era of Reconstruction,* p. 15.
17. Stampp, *The Era of Reconstruction,* p. 202.
18. Woodward, *The Strange Career of Jim Crow,* p. 7.

Chapter 2: Daily Life Under Jim Crow

19. Woodward, *The Strange Career of Jim Crow,* pp. 18–19.
20. Sarah Delany and A. Elizabeth Delany with Amy Hill Hearth, *Having Our Say: The Delany Sisters' First One Hundred Years.* New York: Kodansha International, 1993, pp. 74–76.
21. Stetson Kennedy, *Jim Crow Guide: The Way It Was.* Boca Raton: Florida Atlantic University Press, 1990, p. 212.
22. Charles S. Johnson, *Patterns of Negro Segregation.* New York: Harper & Brothers, 1943, p. 133.
23. Quoted in Litwack, *Trouble in Mind,* p. 336.
24. Quoted in Kennedy, *Jim Crow Guide,* p. 219.
25. Quoted in Johnson, *Patterns of Negro Segregation,* p. 133.
26. Quoted in Johnson, *Patterns of Negro Segregation,* p. 73.
27. Quoted in Milton Meltzer, ed., *The Black Americans: A History in Their Own Words, 1619–1983.* New York: Thomas Y. Crowell, 1984, p. 146.

28. Quoted in Johnson, *Patterns of Negro Segregation*, p. 62.
29. Jim Bishop, *The Days of Martin Luther King Jr.* New York: G. P. Putnam's Sons, 1971, p. 92.
30. Johnson, *Patterns of Negro Segregation*, p. 28.
31. Johnson, *Patterns of Negro Segregation*, pp. 48–49.
32. Jacob Javits, *Discrimination U.S.A.* New York: Harcourt, Brace, 1960, p. 235.
33. Clifton L. Taulbert, *Once upon a Time When We Were Colored*. Tulsa, OK: Council Oak Books, 1989, pp. 105–106.
34. Quoted in Litwack, *Trouble in Mind*, p. 380.
35. Neil R. McMillen, *Dark Journey: Black Mississippians in the Age of Jim Crow*. Urbana: University of Illinois Press, 1989, p. 11.
36. Johnson, *Patterns of Negro Segregation*, p. 77.
37. Litwack, *Trouble in Mind*, p. 236.
38. Quoted in Lynne Ianniello, ed., *Milestones Along the March: Twelve Historic Civil Rights Documents—from World War II to Selma*. New York: Frederick A. Praeger, 1965, pp. 75–76.

Chapter 3: Jim Crow Schools

39. Quoted in Kennedy, *Jim Crow Guide*, p. 86.
40. Quoted in McMillen, *Dark Journey*, p. 72.
41. Kay Mills, *This Little Light of Mine: The Life of Fannie Lou Hamer*. New York: Dutton, 1993, p. 12.
42. Litwack, *Trouble in Mind*, p. 64.
43. Quoted in Walton, *Mississippi*, p. 215.
44. Quoted in Mills, *This Little Light of Mine*, p. 13.
45. Litwack, *Trouble in Mind*, p. 71.
46. Taulbert, *Once upon a Time When We Were Colored*, p. 27.
47. Quoted in Walton, *Mississippi*, p. 215.
48. Quoted in Litwack, *Trouble in Mind*, p. 68.
49. Litwack, *Trouble in Mind*, p. 69.
50. Litwack, *Trouble in Mind*, p. 52.
51. Johnson, *Patterns of Negro Segregation*, p. 197.
52. Quoted in Johnson, *Patterns of Negro Segregation*, pp. 197–98.
53. Quoted in McMillen, *Dark Journey*, p. 72.
54. Quoted in Walton, *Mississippi*, p. 241.

Chapter 4: On the Job

55. Quoted in Kennedy, *Jim Crow Guide*, pp. 119–20.
56. Quoted in Meltzer, *The Black Americans*, p. 226.
57. Du Bois, *The Souls of Black Folk*, p. 119.
58. Martin Luther King Jr., *Why We Can't Wait*. New York: Harper & Row, 1963, p. 41.
59. Quoted in Johnson, *Patterns of Negro Segregation*, p. 204.
60. Quoted in Litwack, *Trouble in Mind*, p. 35.
61. Quoted in Walton, *Mississippi*, pp. 219–21.
62. Quoted in Litwack, *Trouble in Mind*, pp. 6–7.
63. King, *Why We Can't Wait*, p. 13.
64. McMillen, *Dark Journey*, p. 159.
65. Quoted in Litwack, *Trouble in Mind*, p. 339.
66. Litwack, *Trouble in Mind*, p. 340.
67. Litwack, *Trouble in Mind*, p. 126.
68. Quoted in Walton, *Mississippi*, p. 75.
69. Quoted in Litwack, *Trouble in Mind*, p. 150.
70. Quoted in Litwack, *Trouble in Mind*, p. 150.

Chapter 5: "And Justice for All"

71. Quoted in Litwack, *Trouble in Mind*, pp. 224–25. Also quoted in Lawrence W. Levine, *Black Culture and Black Consciousness: Afro American Folk Thought from Slavery to Freedom.* New York: Oxford University Press, 1977, p. 319.
72. Quoted in Litwack, *Trouble in Mind*, p. 226.
73. Quoted in Kennedy, *Jim Crow Guide*, p. 158.
74. Quoted in Mills, *This Little Light of Mine*, pp. 1 2.
75. Quoted in Kennedy, *Jim Crow Guide*, p. 150.
76. Quoted in Kennedy, *Jim Crow Guide*, p. 151.
77. Quoted in Kennedy, *Jim Crow Guide*, p. 158.
78. Quoted in Kennedy, *Jim Crow Guide*, p. 159.
79. Archer, *Growing Up Black in Rural Mississippi*, p. 125.
80. King, *Why We Can't Wait*, pp. 17–18.
81. Litwack, *Trouble in Mind*, p. 307.
82. Quoted in Litwack, *Trouble in Mind*, p. 284.
83. Woodward, *The Strange Career of Jim Crow*, p. 20.
84. Litwack, *Trouble in Mind*, p. 259.
85. Quoted in Litwack, *Trouble in Mind*, pp. 253–54.
86. Litwack, *Trouble in Mind*, p. 252.
87. Du Bois, *The Souls of Black Folk*, p. 123.

Epilogue: The Civil Rights Movement and the End of Jim Crow

88. Quoted in Woodward, *The Strange Career of Jim Crow*, p. 136.
89. Quoted in Wilma Dykeman and James Stokely, *Neither Black nor White.* New York: Rinehart, 1957, p. 165.
90. Quoted in Woodward, *The Strange Career of Jim Crow*, p. 147.
91. Quoted in Ianniello, *Milestones Along the March*, pp. 73–74.
92. Quoted in Coretta Scott King, ed., *The Words of Martin Luther King.* New York: Newmarket, 1983, p. 33.

For Further Reading

Zita Allen, *Black Women Leaders of the Civil Rights Movement*. Danbury, CT: Franklin Watts, 1996. A study of the role women played in the movement—largely unknown and behind the scenes. It is as much about the struggle for gender equality as for racial equality.

Melba Patillo Beals, *Warriors Don't Cry: A Searing Memoir of the Battle to Integrate Little Rock's Central High*. Ed. Anne Greenberg. New York: Archway, 1995. This is the memoir of one of the nine black students who first integrated Central High. It is based on Beals's schoolgirl diary and her mother's notes from the time.

Timothy Levi Biel, *Life in the North During the Civil War*. San Diego: Lucent Books, 1997. Covers the Civil War years in the North. One section focuses on the racial attitudes in the North and the South.

Sara Bullard, *Free at Last: A History of the Civil Rights Movement and Those Who Died in the Struggle*. New York: Oxford University Press, 1993. A chronological study of the civil rights movement. The last section contains biographical sketches of forty people, both black and white, who were part of the movement. It also contains a bibliography.

Kerry Candaele et al., eds., *Bound for Glory: From the Great Migration to the Harlem Renaissance, 1910–1930*. New York: Chelsea House, 1997. A definitive study of African American history in the early twentieth century. It focuses on the black migration from the South to the industrial cities of the North and features the contributions of Louis Armstrong, Satchel Paige, Marcus Garvey, and Langston Hughes.

Ed Clayton, *Martin Luther King: The Peaceful Warrior*. Ed. Pat MacDonald. New York: Archway, 1996. A popular biography of Martin Luther King Jr., it introduces young readers to his philosophy and achievements. Attractively illustrated and readable.

Fred J. Cook, *The Ku Klux Klan: America's Recurring Nightmare*. Morristown, NJ: J. Messner, 1989. A readable account of the history of the KKK, with plenty of photographs. It explores patterns of racial bigotry, religious intolerance, and exploitation. It contains a bibliography and an index.

Michael L. Cooper, *The Double V Campaign: African-Americans and World War II*. New York: Lodestar Books, 1998. A study of the battles fought by African American troops during the war, focusing on the Ninety-second Division in Europe and the Ninety-third Division in the Pacific. Also discusses the racism they faced when they returned home.

Scott Gillam, *Discrimination: Prejudice in Action*. Springfield, NJ: Enslow, 1995. A history of discrimination and ways to deal with it.

Michael Golay, *Reconstruction and Reaction: The Emancipation of Slaves, 1861–1913*. New York: Facts On File, 1996. An anthology of documents associated with African American achievements during and after Reconstruction.

Joy Hakim, *An Age of Extremes*. New York: Oxford University Press, 1994. Part of a well-written, well-organized, and well-illustrated history of the United States. This volume covers the period between 1880 and World War I.

————, *Reconstruction and Reform*. New York: Oxford University Press, 1994. Part of a well-written, well-organized, and well-illustrated history of the United States. This volume covers the period from just after the Civil War to the beginning of the twentieth century.

James Haskins, *Bayard Rustin: Behind the Scenes of the Civil Rights Movement*. Winnipeg, Manitoba, Canada: Hyperion, 1997. A moving and inspirational story about a relatively unknown leader of the civil rights movement. Controversial because of his homosexuality and communism, Rustin organized the 1963 March on Washington. The book covers fifty years of events that shaped Rustin's commitment to the civil rights cause.

————, *Separate, but Not Equal: The Dream and the Struggle*. New York: Scholastic, 1998. Background on the history of African Americans' struggle for equal rights in education, from slavery to affirmative action. Landmark court cases are discussed in detail as well as the philosophies of W. E. B. Du Bois and Booker T. Washington. Few illustrations, but a wealth of facts and statistics as well as a bibliography and index.

Debra Hess, *Thurgood Marshall: The Fight for Equal Justice*. Englewood Cliffs, NJ: Silver Burdett, 1990. A biography of Marshall, focusing on his landmark Supreme Court case for the NAACP and his later appointment to the Supreme Court.

Mary Hull, *Rosa Parks*. New York: Chelsea House, 1994. A biography of the civil rights leader.

Stuart A. Kallen, *The Twentieth Century and the Harlem Renaissance: A History of Black People in America, 1880–1930*. Edina, MN: Abdo and Daughters, 1990. Black history in the early decades of the twentieth century. Profiles of W. E. B. Du Bois, Booker T. Washington, Langston Hughes, and Louis Armstrong.

Deborah Kent, *Thurgood Marshall and the Supreme Court*. Danbury, CT: Childrens Press, 1997. A clear, simple text about the legal leader of the NAACP and later Supreme Court justice. It includes plenty of photographs and a timeline.

Casey King, *Oh, Freedom!: Kids Talk About the Civil Rights Movement with the People Who Made It Happen*. New York: Knopf, 1997. Contains a foreword by Rosa Parks. Part traditional history, part oral history, kids interview everyday people about their involvement in the movement. Well illustrated and includes a bibliography of books, videos, and recordings.

Pat McKissack et al., *The Civil Rights Movement in America: From 1865 to the Present*. Danbury, CT: Childrens Press, 1991. Traces the black struggle from Reconstruction to the present, comparing African Americans' struggle to that of other minorities.

Zak Mettger, *Reconstruction: America After the Civil War*. New York: Lodestar Books, 1994. A well-written account, using historical documents and firsthand accounts of former slaves and slave owners. It emphasizes the legislative maneuvering of southern states to deny blacks their civil rights. Contains clear, concise explanations, a glossary, bibliography, and plenty of illustrations.

Gerald Newman and Eleanor Newman Layfield, *Racism: Divided by Color*. Springfield, NJ: Enslow, 1995. A history of racism and how to deal with it. Contains a bibliography, glossary, and index.

Michael Newton, *Walking for Freedom: The Montgomery Bus Boycott*. Chatham, NJ:

Raintree/Steck Vaughn, 1996. Part of a series edited by Alex Haley, the author of *Roots*. The book uses personal anecdotes to explain the event.

Laurie A. O'Neill, *Little Rock: The Desegregation of Central High*. Brookfield, CT: Millbrook, 1994. Vivid and dramatic stories of the nine black students who first integrated Central High. Well illustrated and containing a bibliography and index.

Angela Phillips, *Discrimination*. Morristown, NJ: New Discovery, 1993. A history of discrimination from A.D. 380 to the present.

Fred Powledge, *We Shall Overcome: Heroes of the Civil Rights Movement*. New York: Scribner, 1993. Presents the personal experiences of ten "ordinary" civil rights workers. Well organized and passionate, it gives the reader insights into what the movement was really like.

Carl Senna, *The Black Press and the Struggle for Civil Rights*. Danbury, CT: Franklin Watts, 1994. A history of the black press and its role in the fight for civil rights.

Lori Shein, *Inequality: Opposing Viewpoints*. San Diego: Greenhaven, 1998. An extensive debate packed with arguments, speeches, and articles supporting both sides of the issue. Useful editorial overviews and commentaries as well as complete footnotes and a bibliography. This will definitely spark discussion.

Robert Weisbrot and Margaret Dornfield, *Marching Toward Freedom, 1957–1965*. New York: Chelsea House, 1994. A coherent, objective look at the civil rights movement from the 1960 sit-in at the Woolworth lunch counter to Little Rock's Central High School and Selma, Alabama. It contains a timeline and bibliography but is short on documentation for the conversations quoted from key events.

Sarah E. Wright, *A. Philip Randolph: Integration in the Workplace*. Englewood Cliffs, NJ: Silver Burdett, 1990. A biography of the civil rights leader with lots of photographs, a bibliography, and an index. It also focuses on the major civil rights organizations of the 1950s and 1960s.

J. William T. Youngs and Bill Youngs, *American Realities: Historical Episodes: From Reconstruction to the Present*. Don Mills, Ontario, Canada: Addison-Wesley, 1997. A 352-page history of America's past 130 years.

Works Consulted

Books

Chalmers Archer Jr., *Growing Up Black in Rural Mississippi: Memories of a Family, Heritage of a Place*. New York: Walker, 1992. Memoirs of growing up black on a small Mississippi farm. Lots of family stories about discrimination as well as strong family and church heritage.

James Baldwin, *Nobody Knows My Name: More Notes of a Native Son*. New York: Dell, 1961. The award-winning author continues his poignant and passionate commentary on being a black American.

Jim Bishop, *The Days of Martin Luther King Jr.* New York: G. P. Putnam's Sons, 1971. An exhaustive biography of Martin Luther King Jr.

Jim Carnes, *Us and Them: A History of Intolerance in America*. Montgomery, AL: Southern Poverty Law Center, 1995. A magazine published by an organization devoted to social equality for all people and an end to discrimination and hate crimes. Excellent overview of racial and cultural prejudice in America from its beginnings to the present day.

Henry Steele Commager, ed., *Documents of American History*. Vol. 1. New York: Appleton-Century-Crofts, 1968. Anthology of famous American documents from 1492 to 1898.

Kenneth C. Davis, *Don't Know Much About History: Everything You Need to Know About American History but Never Learned*. New York: Avon Books, 1990. A humorous yet highly informative compilation of facts and anecdotes from American history—from the arrival of Columbus to the Iran-Contra affair. It explodes long-held myths and misconceptions and is a handy reference book.

Sarah Delany and A. Elizabeth Delany with Amy Hill Hearth, *Having Our Say: The Delany Sisters' First One Hundred Years*. New York: Kodansha International, 1993. Autobiographical accounts by two aged black sisters who first experienced racism as small children in the 1880s and watched the changes that occurred during their century of life.

W. E. B. Du Bois, *The Souls of Black Folk*. 1903. Reprint, New York: Bantam, 1989. Classic work on the essence of being black in America. Philosophical basis for much of the civil rights movement and the black consciousness movement.

Wilma Dykeman and James Stokely, *Neither Black nor White*. New York: Rinehart, 1957. Hundreds of personal interviews of southerners, both black and white, about the South, race relations, the civil rights movement, and key events in southern history.

David Frost Jr., *Witness to Injustice*. Jackson: University Press of Mississippi, 1995. Memoirs of growing up black in Mississippi during the first half of the twentieth century.

John Howard Griffin, *Black Like Me*. New York: Signet, 1960. The incredible story of a white journalist who dyed his skin black, shaved his head, and traveled throughout the segregated South in the 1960s to experience life as a black man.

Lynne Ianniello, ed., *Milestones Along the March: Twelve Historic Civil Rights Documents—from World War II to Selma*.

New York: Frederick A. Praeger, 1965. Anthology of important documents covering the years of the civil rights movement.

Jacob Javits, *Discrimination, U.S.A.* New York: Harcourt, Brace, 1960. An in-depth study of racial discrimination in the United States by the former senator from New York.

Peter Jennings and Todd Brewster, *The Century.* New York: ABC Television Network Group/Doubleday, 1998. Includes an extensive chapter covering the civil rights movement and segregation.

Charles S. Johnson, *Patterns of Negro Segregation.* New York: Harper & Brothers, 1943. An exhaustive report on segregation based on a study of randomly selected southern cities and towns. Hundreds of first-person interviews and objective on-site observations.

Stetson Kennedy, *Jim Crow Guide: The Way It Was.* Boca Raton: Florida Atlantic University Press, 1990. Written as a guidebook for persons experiencing the Jim Crow South. Very comprehensive, with detailed accounts of segregation and an abundance of statistics dealing with race relations.

Coretta Scott King, *My Life with Martin Luther King.* New York: Avon Books, 1969. Autobiographical memoir by Martin Luther King Jr.'s widow. Full of inspirational images and anecdotes from their life together and the fascinating people they met.

Coretta Scott King, ed., *The Words of Martin Luther King.* New York: Newmarket, 1983. A compilation of quotations from King's writings, interviews, sermons, and speeches chosen by his widow.

Martin Luther King Jr., *Why We Can't Wait.* New York: Harper & Row, 1963. Philosophical basis for and explanation of King's nonviolent civil resistance to discrimination.

Lawrence W. Levine, *Black Culture and Black Consciousness: Afro American Folk Thought from Slavery to Freedom.* New York: Oxford University Press, 1977. Weighty but readable, this book focuses on African American oral traditions, encompassing sacred and secular music, folktales, humor, and legends. Includes many examples to support each point made.

Leon F. Litwack, *Trouble in Mind: Black Southerners in the Age of Jim Crow.* New York: Alfred A. Knopf, 1998. The definitive source on the Jim Crow era. The Pultzer Prize–winning historian draws on a vast array of contemporary documents and first-person narratives from both blacks and whites. Includes hundreds of footnotes, an incredible bibliography, and an extensive index.

Chris Mayfield, ed., *Growing Up Southern: Southern Exposure Looks at Childhood.* New York: Pantheon Books, 1976. A collection of articles from *Southern Exposure* magazine, covering a wide range of southern customs and attitudes.

Neil R. McMillen, *Dark Journey: Black Mississippians in the Age of Jim Crow.* Urbana: University of Illinois Press, 1989. A complete, in-depth study of the Jim Crow years in Mississippi. Contains hundreds of personal accounts.

Milton Meltzer, *Freedom Comes to Mississippi: The Story of Reconstruction.* Chicago: Follett, 1970. Historical background on Reconstruction and how it specifically affected Mississippi's black and white population.

Milton Meltzer, ed., *The Black Americans: A History in Their Own Words, 1619–1983.* New York: Thomas Y. Crowell, 1984. Anthology of writings by black Americans, from slave diaries to participants in the civil rights movement.

Kay Mills, *This Little Light of Mine: The Life of Fannie Lou Hamer*. New York: Dutton, 1993. An intimate, thorough biography of the Mississippi civil rights leader who went from sharecropping to politics.

Anne Moody, *Coming of Age in Mississippi*. New York: Dial, 1968. Autobiography of a young black girl struggling with racism, the Ku Klux Klan, and white violence. Includes stories about activities during the years of the civil rights movement.

Rosa Parks with Jim Haskins, *Rosa Parks: My Story*. New York: Dial Books, 1992. Personal memoirs of "the Mother of the Modern Civil Rights Movement." Relates the story of her parents, her childhood in Alabama, her experiences during the Jim Crow era, her participation in the civil rights movement, and her life since. Includes a chronology and index.

Thomas F. Pettigrew, "Segregation," *World Book Encyclopedia*. Vol. 17. Chicago: Field Enterprises Educational, 1977. Basic information on the types of segregation, both in the United States and around the world.

John Shelton Reed and Dale Volberg Reed, *1001 Things Everyone Should Know About the South*. New York: Doubleday, 1996. A readable, interesting collection of facts and stories about the South. This well-organized, concise book offers dozens of biographical sketches of important southerners.

Kenneth M. Stampp, *The Era of Reconstruction: 1865–1877*. New York: Vintage Books, 1965. A comprehensive study of the Reconstruction era containing plenty of personal accounts both from blacks and from whites.

Tracy Sugarman, *Stranger at the Gates: A Summer in Mississippi*. New York: Hill and Wang, 1966. Memoirs of a northern journalist who came to the South during the Freedom Summer of 1964.

Clifton L. Taulbert, *Once upon a Time When We Were Colored*. Tulsa, OK: Council Oak Books, 1989. Personal memoirs of growing up black in a small rural Mississippi town. Includes touching narratives told to the author by older relatives who remember what life was like under slavery and just after Reconstruction.

Anthony Walton, *Mississippi: An American Journey*. New York: Vintage Books, 1996. Recollections of a black childhood in Mississippi as well as a travelogue of a trip taken across the state as an adult. Includes several interesting family anecdotes and in-depth local history.

Booker T. Washington, *Up from Slavery*. New York: Bantam Books, 1900. The autobiography of the famous educator, statesman, and scholar.

Diana Wells, comp., *We Have a Dream: African-American Visions of Freedom*. New York: Carrol & Graff/Richard Gallen, 1993. An anthology of works (speeches, articles, excerpts, and essays) by black writers, centering on the struggle for civil rights.

C. Vann Woodward, *The Strange Career of Jim Crow*. 3rd ed. New York: Oxford University Press, 1974. Probably the most widely quoted book on Jim Crow, it offers a well-organized and in-depth treatment of the origins and practices of the Jim Crow system.

Andrew Young, *An Easy Burden: The Civil Rights Movement and the Transformation of America*. Norwalk, CT: Easton, 1996. Memoirs of personal experiences during the civil rights movement, work with

Martin Luther King Jr., and King's opinion about the movement's effectiveness and the country's racial outlook.

Periodicals

Edmundo Castro, "Jim Crow Laws: Stricken from the Books but Still Enforced," *Sunset Freedom,* October 1996. Extensive article about the history of Jim Crow laws and how many of the same restrictions still apply to black people. The author cites ample statistics to back up his claims.

Major W. Cox, "Path of Racial Discrimination Ends with Criminal Statutes," *Montgomery Advertiser,* December 17, 1997. Article about the criminal justice system in the United States and its treatment of blacks.

Index

Picture Credits

About the Author

Charles George was born and raised in a small town in western Texas. Growing up during the 1950s and 1960s, he experienced firsthand some aspects of the Jim Crow system. After graduating from Tarleton State University with a degree in Spanish and history, George taught in Texas public high schools for fifteen years. Most recently he was head of the Social Studies Department at Early High School in central Texas, but he has since taken a break from the classroom to write full time with Linda, his wife of twenty-eight years.

Together, they have written over thirty young adult and children's non-fiction books in the past two years, including two that dealt with the civil rights movement. This is his first book for Lucent Books.